THE MAGIC & MYSTERY OF THE
LAKE DISTRICT

Biographies and Acknowledgements

Photographs by David W. Jones and E. A. Bowness:

For Michael and Alison
David W. Jones moved to the Lake District in 1964. Gaining inspiration from classes on
Industrial Archaeology, David took up black and white photography, selling his first pictures
to Cumbria magazine. Later his field of interest extended to include traditional Lakeland
scenes. In 1980, David's book A Lakeland Camera was published. He has also held several
exhibitions of his photographs.

For my wife Christine and son John
Ted Bowness was born into an old Lake District family in Langdale, and now lives in a
South Lakeland village. He sold his first photograph to Motorcycle Magazine in 1949 whilst
a student at Manchester, before graduating in geography. He later established his own
picture library of Cumbria, producing a colour book in 1978, which has sold over 100,000
copies. He has dedicated this book to his wife and son, to thank them for accepting his
many excursions 'going out with the cameras'.

Text by Lucinda Hawksley and Dorothy Jones:

For my grandparents and for Eleanor
Lucinda Hawksley is based in London but has enjoyed many memorable holidays in the
Lake District. A literature graduate, she has studied the works of Wordsworth and Coleridge
in detail and is currently working towards a post-graduate thesis in literature and history of art.

For Michael and Alison
Dorothy Jones moved to the southern fringe of the Lake District with her photographer husband, David, in 1964. When David's photography branched out into illustrated articles for
various magazines, the texts were provided by Dorothy.

With grateful thanks to Helen Courtney who designed this book, also to Lesley Malkin, Ezra
Nathan and Sonya Newland for editorial work and to Anna Newland and Henry Hawksley
for help with the research.

All pictures courtesy of David W. Jones and E. A. Bowness,
except for page 197 courtesy of The Bridgeman Art Library.

ISBN 1 84084 163 X

First published in 1998 by
DEMPSEY PARR
13 Whiteladies Road
Clifton Bristol BS8 1PB

Copyright 1998 © Dempsey Parr

Produced for Dempsey Parr by Foundry Design and Production,
The Long House, Antrobus Road, Chiswick, London W4 5HY.

THE MAGIC & MYSTERY OF THE
LAKE DISTRICT

PHOTOGRAPHS BY DAVID W. JONES & E. A. BOWNESS

David W Jones. *Ted Bowness*

Text by Lucinda Hawksley & Dorothy Jones

DP
DEMPSEY
PARR

Contents

Contents by Region

INTRODUCTION

England's Lake District holds an unassailable fascination for all who have known it. Breathtaking views, rich traditions, unrivalled landscapes and prolific literary and artistic associations combine to create an atmosphere of vibrant originality. Known by a variety of names: the Lake District, Lakeland, the Lakes or the English Lakes; this region has enticed visitors for many centuries.

The origins of the lakes and valleys in this area date back to Britain's last ice age. When the glaciers began to melt, water began to cascade down mountain sides, creating the horseshoe passes so definitive of Cumbrian scenery, as well as the lakes, rivers, bays and valleys we know today.

The first settlers in the Lake District arrived about 5000 years ago. They lived in what are now seen as unfeasibly high settlements, way up on the fells. Archaeologists have discovered many relics of these long-gone communities, including graves, stone circles, axes and carvings. The reason they lived at this high altitude was the impenetrability of the lower land. Unforgiving trees and dense undergrowth created an insuperable barrier to living in the valleys, as did the wild beasts that inhabited these lowlands. It was for this reason that the famed Roman road, known today simply as 'High Street' came to be built 823 metres up, spanning the distance between ancient forts at Ambleside (Galava) and Brougham (Brocavum). After the Romans came ninth- and tenth-century Norse settlers, and the area has also suffered periodic invasions from Scotland.

Before 1974, the area now called Cumbria was actually several different counties: Cumberland, Westmorland, northern Lancashire and the West Riding district of Yorkshire. These four regions all enjoyed a great many local traditions and rich independent histories.

Visitors to Lakeland are regularly treated to this diversity of culture as throughout the year there are myriad fascinating local entertainments, many of which originated centuries ago. These include the annual rushbearing ceremonies that take place in

Grasmere and Ambleside during the summer months. Rushbearing harks back to a time when church floors were made simply of earth, covered with a mat of rushes. On an appointed day, the floors would be swept clean of the previous year's much trodden covering and spread with newly cut rushes. The children of Ambleside and Grasmere join in these celebrations with great excitement, wearing ornate head-dresses of freshly bound flowers.

Another tradition dates back, allegedly, to biblical times. Cumberland and

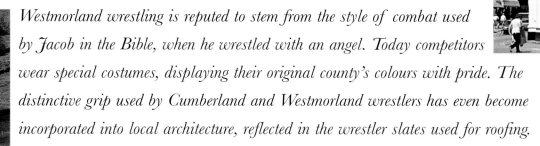

Westmorland wrestling is reputed to stem from the style of combat used by Jacob in the Bible, when he wrestled with an angel. Today competitors wear special costumes, displaying their original county's colours with pride. The distinctive grip used by Cumberland and Westmorland wrestlers has even become incorporated into local architecture, reflected in the wrestler slates used for roofing.

Wrestling, an essentially Cumbrian sport, was an important part of military training in the Middle Ages and, in the eighteenth century, was considered an indispensable skill for fencers and duellists. Today, competitions are held throughout Lakeland from August to October.

Another local tradition takes place at Easter, yet its origins lie in pagan religions of pre-Christian times. As happened with many pagan ceremonies, this one was assimilated into the Christian year. Today, at Penrith, one can watch the Easter Monday tradition of egg-rolling. Eggs are first hard-boiled and dyed in bright colours, then the contestants stand at the top of Castlemont Hill and send their eggs rolling to the bottom. The winner is determined by the egg that rolls furthest or survives the greatest number of trips. Other egg-rolling competitions take place at Edinburgh's Arthur's Seat, Derby's Bunkers Hill and Preston's Avenham Park; the ritual was originally a pagan solar rite but, post-Christianity, has come to symbolize the rolling away of the stone at the entrance to Jesus' tomb.

As well as being an area of great natural beauty and ancient traditions, Lakeland is perhaps most renowned for its famous inhabitants. Something about the region seems to instil

artistic brilliance into its people. William and Dorothy Wordsworth spent almost all their lives here and their presence is echoed in the homes they shared and the land immortalized in their writings. The Wordsworths' great friend, Samuel Taylor Coleridge, best known as the author of the epic poem, The Rime of the Ancient Mariner, also lived here; as did his son, a famous writer in his own right, Hartley Coleridge. Thomas De Quincey, Matthew Arnold, Arthur Ransome, Robert Southey, Michael Drayton, Hugh Walpole and John Ruskin all lived and wrote in the Lake District and Charles Dickens and Wilkie Collins made a memorable (and much loathed) visit here in 1857, a hilarious trip recreated in their joint essay The Lazy Tour of Two Idle Apprentices. As well as these illustrious men, the name of the district's favourite daughter must be recorded: Beatrix Potter, the remarkable woman whose works and memory rival William Wordsworth's for local adulation. Few authors have captured the imagination and hearts of children the world over as Beatrix Potter managed to do in her magical texts. Based on an in-depth knowledge of the area, an undying love of nature and prodigious illustrative skills, Potter's series of animal stories have delighted generations since her first novel 'The Tale of Peter Rabbit' was published in 1900. Beatrix Potter's life and works are commemorated in several museums around Lakeland,

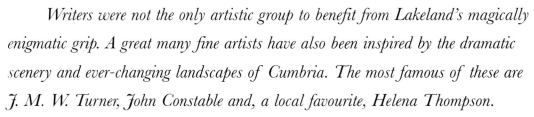

as are the lives and works of William Wordsworth, poet extraordinaire, and his journal-writing sister, Dorothy.

Writers were not the only artistic group to benefit from Lakeland's magically enigmatic grip. A great many fine artists have also been inspired by the dramatic scenery and ever-changing landscapes of Cumbria. The most famous of these are J. M. W. Turner, John Constable and, a local favourite, Helena Thompson.

The Lake District encompasses 880 square miles of land, though it measures just 30 miles across. It is a designated National Park, the largest area of such parkland in the country, and has become one of the most commonly visited districts of the British Isles. The first steady trickle of tourists to this area began to arrive in the late eighteenth and early nineteenth centuries. The French Revolution of 1789, followed by decades of swirling unrest, had a huge effect on British tourist patterns: those who would have previously journeyed to the Continent for honeymoons or holidays were frightened by the escalating stories of French brutalities and citizen uprisings. Inevitably, travellers began to look to their own islands and the Lakes became one of the key places to visit.

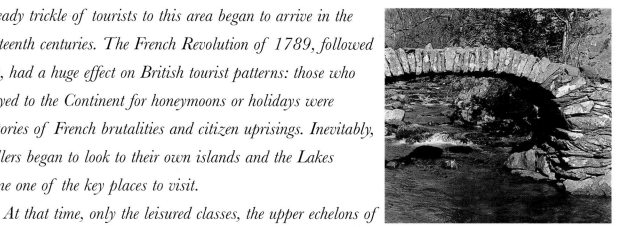

At that time, only the leisured classes, the upper echelons of British society, could afford the time and money to travel habitually. As a result, prior to the mid-nineteenth century, Lakeland's visitors were a genteel assembly of the privileged minority. It was in 1844, when the first plans for a railway extension to Kendal were unveiled, that the face of the Lake District began to change. The railway was vehemently opposed by the locals, most vociferously by the then Poet Laureate, William Wordsworth, but their objections were over-ruled. Today the railways and roads convey upwards of 18 million people to the region every year; roughly equivalent to one-third of the population of Britain.

John Ruskin, another prominent Lakeland dweller, also dreaded a tourist invasion. He wrote of the impending influx of the lower classes: I do not want them to see Helvellyn when they are drunk. Today his house, Brantwood, near Coniston, is open for the twentieth-century's hordes of tourists to view. It is a remarkable house and a well-preserved monument to its equally remarkable owner.

William and Dorothy Wordsworth, together with Samuel Taylor Coleridge, tended towards Pantheism, a form of deeply felt Christianity where God is perceived as present in all elements of nature. This strong belief is echoed in the writings of all three. When surveying the surroundings in which they spent their lives, it is very easy to empathize with their creed.

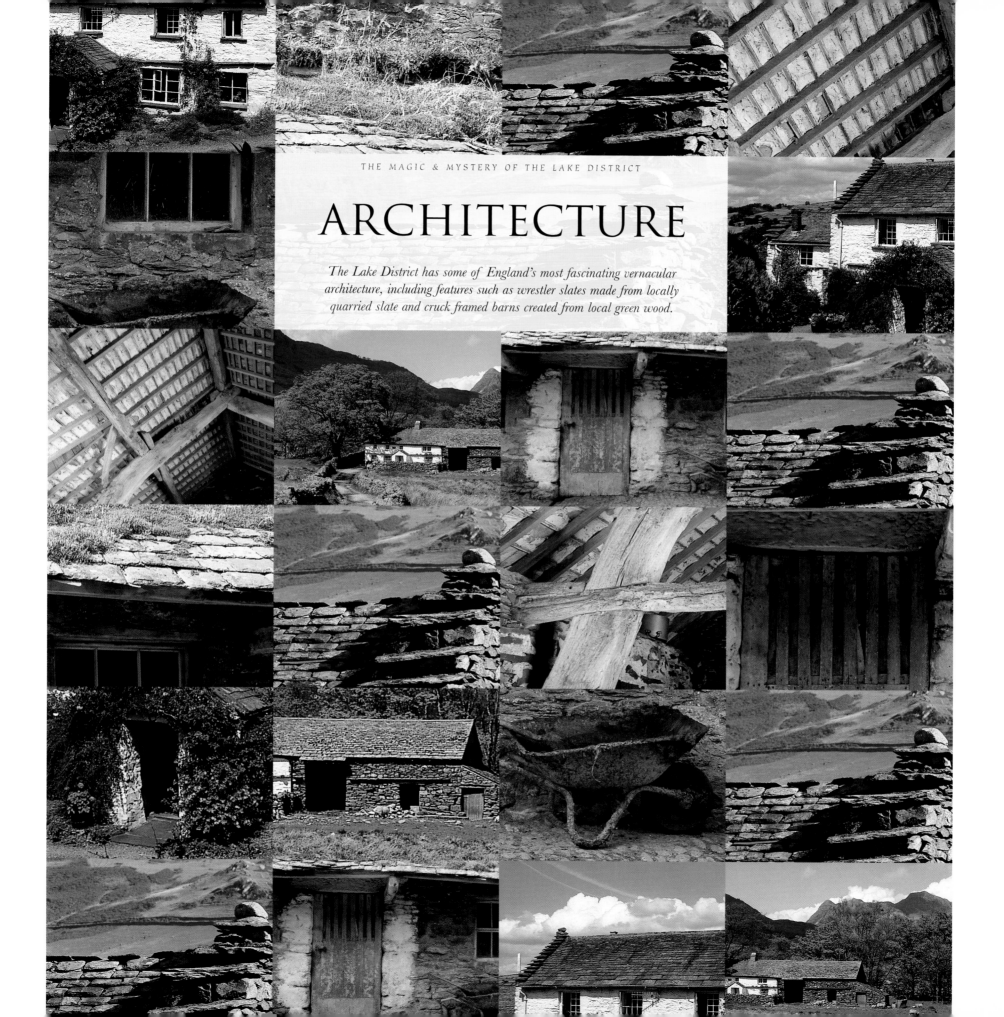

ARCHITECTURE

The Lake District has some of England's most fascinating vernacular architecture, including features such as wrestler slates made from locally quarried slate and cruck framed barns created from local green wood.

Traditional Bank Barn
NEAR GRANGE-OVER-SANDS

Lakeland slate is a most attractive environment for lichens and plants. After many years, if undisturbed, plants such as Biting Stonecrop may colonize, spreading out roots with little damage to the slate beneath.

Canopy roofs afford protection from the worst of the elements. They are not built to give the farmer a place to shelter but to partly cover the half-open doors beneath. Cow byres and stables are found behind these doors and as animals need good ventilation, they are commonly split or the upper part slatted. Although air is free to enter and leave, rain and snow are not. The walls are frequently rendered or doorways marked in white. This was possibly to help the farmer on dark mornings in the days before electricity.

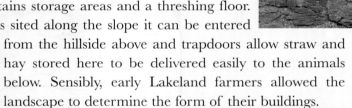

Above the canopy is the upper storey of the bank barn, which contains storage areas and a threshing floor. As the building is sited along the slope it can be entered from the hillside above and trapdoors allow straw and hay stored here to be delivered easily to the animals below. Sensibly, early Lakeland farmers allowed the landscape to determine the form of their buildings.

Wrestler Slates
TROUTBECK

After 1650 there were no timber-framed houses of note built in the Lake District. For the following 100 years a 'Great Rebuilding' took place. The new houses were built of stone and their walls were strong enough to bear a roof of slate. As slate quarrying had taken place for centuries there was much to be had, but it did require splitting and was hard to work.

Roof slates were laid in diminishing courses, larger wider slates at the eves and shorter narrower ones at the ridge. They were rounded at the head and squared at the foot and were fixed to laths with an oak peg. The ridge could be clothed in more

easily worked stone, shaped to fit, or with wrestler slates. These wrestler slates were cut to interlock, the name being descriptive of the popular Cumberland and Westmorland sport of wrestling. They proved more than a match for the wind and rain but are now rarely to be found.

Crow-stepped gables, built as part of the gable end, prevent the lifting of slates and protect the eves. The steps slope slightly to shed the rain and finish with a 'kneeler'. They were considered to be decorative in the nineteenth century and were sometimes added for aesthetic reasons.

Fusthwaite Yeat
TROUTBECK

Even though the original mullioned windows no longer adorn this house it is still a very pretty cottage. Many of its features are picturesque: round chimneys, crow stepped gables, dripstones and white-rendered walls with garden flowers growing in front.

Inside are many original features including the doors, and a court cupboard. Oak partitioning is common in small farmhouses such as these, and the court cupboard was built into this partitioning, opposite the main fire. These cupboards were used to store quantities of home-baked oat clapbread, and for family valuables such as pewter, silver and spirits. Here, the cupboard rises from floor to ceiling in three stages. The top stage is elaborately carved and bears the date 1683 and the initials of the original owner. The lower stages are free of decoration for they would receive the wear and tear of daily living.

Outside, the round chimney projects from the gable wall at first-floor level. Once a lath and plaster hood would have been found in the upper chamber, carrying smoke from the fire below. A large porch shelters the door and offered the farmer a place to leave his boots.

Bridge End Farm
LITTLE LANGDALE

Bridge End Farm can now be described as being 'off the beaten track' but it was once on the road through the valley to Wrynose Pass. Not only has the road been re-routed but the farmhouse itself is no longer needed as a farmhouse as the land is now farmed by farmers nearby. The National Trust therefore rents this property to holidaymakers, who can enjoy the rural scene in peace.

The farm has been much altered during its lifetime, but it still retains many traditional characteristics. If you enter the house through the porch you will find yourself in a wood-panelled passage known as a

hallen. To your left, the original main room houses a court or bread cupboard. A tiny fire window (now enlarged) illuminates the fireside. A spice cupboard would once have been set into the wall by the fire. To the right of the hallen is the downhouse, once used for brewing, baking and other domestic tasks. The upper rooms would have originally been reached by a ladder.

In common with many farmsteads built at this time, shelter was more important than the view, but the magnificent Langdale Pikes can be seen from the back of the building.

Yanwath Hall
NEAR PENRITH

The tower at Yanwath Hall was built in response to the Scottish raiders who came south seeking goods and livestock. Built in the fourteenth century, it is a simple three-storey rectangle with high windows and a roof from which watch could be kept. A sturdy door and iron grille would give added security. When warning came of attack the family and tenants would withdraw into the tower, the thick walls of which were sufficient to withstand a short siege. The hope was that the attackers would leave for easier pickings.

In 1463 Edward IV made a truce with Scotland and the area became more settled. In 1575 Sir Lancelot Threlkeld considered his house near Penrith 'a place of profit and warmth for the winter'. When times were more settled still, the addition of domestic buildings with a central hall flanked by two-storey wings added greatly to the comfort of the inhabitants and although we might consider these quarters cold by modern standards, they were much admired in their day. The protective encircling wall has been reduced in height and a garden now replaces what was once an area of sanctuary.

Studded Door
BORROWDALE

The door forms one of the first impressions of a home and this door, with its beautiful latch and studs, shows fine workmanship. You can see the wood is strong and the wooden studs tell us that it is a double door. The outside planks are vertical and the inside ones horizontal, which gives extra strength. They are joined firmly together by faceted pegs. The only wood for such an important door is oak. Such a heavy door would have been hung originally on strap hinges fastened against the wooden door surround.

This door is to be found in Borrowdale at Ashness Farm. It is part of a substantial statesman's house – a term used instead of yeoman – and is an indication of the fine appointment and size of the interior rooms. It reflects the wealth and status of a farmer with substantial land holdings and large numbers of livestock.

Cruck Frame Barn
HAWKSHEAD

Cruck frame construction is simple and effective. All the weight of the roof is borne by these impressive timbers, which rest on the earth floor of the building, the end of the cruck being set on stones to prevent rotting.

Landlords guarded their timber jealously and tenants had to prove their need for the valuable oak or supply their own. Trees had to be felled then split in two to form the perfectly balanced arch. They were cut just as the sap was rising and the bark was stripped and sold by the owner. The green wood was then used without being seasoned. The cruck barn dates from medieval times when tools were mainly the adze and axe, which gave a wonderful finish to the wood.

Once erected, the tie-beam added strength and crossed between the crucks at the level of the wall. A feature called a blade was grooved and a timber known as a purlin set into it, joining the sets of crucks together and giving rigidity. The size of barn depended on the number of crucks. It was always single storey and placed on level ground. On the roof the two blades were lap-jointed together and sometimes notched for the ridge piece. Coppiced poles were split to make laths, which secured the heavy slate roof, thus protecting the dry-stone walls and the animals housed within.

BRIDGES

As well as myriad lakes, the Lake District also has many fast-flowing rivers over which a variety of bridges stand. Throughout history many illustrious persons have crossed Lakeland's turbulent waters by means of these bridges.

Skelwith Bridge
RIVER BRATHAY

Thomas De Quincey often visited the River Brathay and spent many hours in contemplation on its banks. Wordsworth also wrote of walks to Brathay and Skelwith Bridge. In his time Skelwith was usually written as 'Skelleth'.

In her journal of June 1800, Dorothy Wordsworth wrote the following:

Wm. and I went to Brathay by Little Langdale and Collath and Skelleth. It was a warm, mild morning with threatening of rain. The vale of Little Langdale looked bare and unlovely. Collath was wild and interesting ... the valley all perfumed with the gale and wild thyme. The woods about the waterfall veined with rich yellow Broom. A succession of delicious views from Skelleth to Brathay.

from the journals of Dorothy Wordsworth

Skelwith Bridge is the crossing point on the River Brathay. It was formerly crossed by a county bridge, which joined the old counties of Westmorland and the Furness district of Lancashire. Today's bridge is a popular spot with walkers on circular routes that cross the river and take them past the well-known Skelwith Waterfall.

Devils Bridge

KIRKBY LONSDALE

A poor old lady living close to the River Lune at Kirkby Lonsdale found her pony and cow stranded on the opposite bank of the river after it had flooded following a storm. The Devil, hearing her cries, offered to build a bridge during the night on the condition that he would possess the first living thing to cross it.

By morning the bridge was complete. The Devil called to the woman to cross over and fetch her animals. Knowing the Devil would try to take her, she took out a bun from her pocket and threw it across the bridge. Her dog ran to retrieve it thus foiling the Devil's plan, who disappeared in a fury together with the dog, leaving the bridge behind.

If this tale is to be believed, the Devil was an excellent bridge builder, and worked here in the late fifteenth or early sixteenth century. The chamfered arches are elegant and simple in style, and the parapets with deep embrasures for pedestrians are in a style more akin to the seventeenth century.

In fact, it is most likely that an early wooden bridge was replaced during the fourteenth century by one of stone, with repairs and alterations made during the following century.

Clapper Bridge
NEAR SOULBY

A clapper bridge is simple in form, crudely constructed and 'rough' in appearance. Placing large slabs of rock across a beck, as here, was the most obvious way, prior to the use of arches in bridge building, to ford a stream.

Very little is known about this clapper bridge, which spans Potts Beck, just inside the parish of Great Ashby at Water House near the village of Soulby. From its appearance we can, however, conclude that it is still functional and very old.

Soulby is a small but spacious settlement on the banks of Scandale Beck. The village name is thought to mean either 'a short valley' or 'a joining of two rivers' and dates back to Norse times. Water played an important role in this rural community. An old water mill stood above the village and was in use until the 1950s. The village pump provided drinking water until 1938, when piped water was connected.

The large village green is used to host sheep and cattle fairs each year. Strangely there are no ancient buildings to point to early settlement. The church dates from 1663, but the bridge would have been in use from an earlier time.

High Sweden Bridge
SCANDALE BECK AMBLESIDE

The delicate stone arch of High Sweden Bridge spans Scandale Beck. The gentle stream that flows beneath falls from the fellside above through steep ravines and changes quickly to become a raging torrent.

Sure-footed pack horses crossed this simple arch, without a parapet, perhaps designed so because of the size of the loads carried. For almost 300 years this bridge has withstood the elements, the classic keystone construction holding firm.

Approached from Ambleside, the view of Coniston Fells, Langdale Pikes and pastures full of wild flowers and charming woodlands, is superb. Above the bridge, drystone walls guide a track upwards to Scandale Pass and over to Brotherswater. Hill walkers cross the bridge to the Fairfield Horseshoe, enjoying the contrasting scenes. An idyllic picnic spot, High Sweden Bridge offers an alternative route back to Ambleside along the beckside, delighting visitors every step of the way.

Grange Bridge
BORROWDALE

The distinctive structure of Grange Bridge dates from 1675. Its frame spans the River Derwent at Grange in Borrowdale, allowing safe passage across often turbulent water. The name Grange was applied to estates or farms owned by monasteries. It comes from the word granary, a vital part of any farm required to provide food for such a large community. In the case of Grange Bridge, the nearby farm was owned by the illustrious Furness Abbey. The bridge was a vital crossing point for monks needing to access land they owned on the other side of the river.

From the time of the Middle Ages most religious orders were also strong agricultural communities, working together to provide food for themselves and the poor of the surrounding area. If they had surplus produce, it was sold to provide some income. Religious orders of the era were wealthy and wielded enormous power over their surrounding parishioners.

Pelter Bridge and Nab Scar
RYDAL

Pelter Bridge at Rydal is part of a minor road that crosses the River Rothay leading to Ambleside, by way of Loughrigg Fell. William Wordsworth spent many years living at Rydal Mount, approximately half a mile away from Pelter Bridge. He must have used it to cross the river a great many times. The snowy hill in the background is Nab Scar, another favourite walk of the Lake Poets. Dorothy wrote about this area in her journal of October 1800:

Rydale was very, very beautiful. The surface of the water quite still, like a dim mirror. The colours of the large island exquisitely beautiful, and the trees still fresh and green were magnified by the mists. The prospects on the west side of the Lake were very beautiful. We sate at the 'two points' looking up to Park's. The lowing of the cattle was echoed by a hollow voice in Knab Scar. We went upon Loughrigg Fell ... We returned home over the stepping stones.

from the journals of
Dorothy Wordsworth

LIVING FROM THE LAND

The Lakeland community has its roots in agriculture and although the district's primary industry is now tourism, the rural traditions of Cumbria's old counties still prevail.

Yew Tree Farm
CONISTON

Hill farms are not suitable for large scale poultry farming: besides shape, the eggs produced would bear little resemblance to the deep golden-yolked eggs of the true free range hen. The farmer's wife is often assigned the task of looking after the hens, and sometimes this grows into an enterprise all of its own. The hens usually roam the farmyard freely. These hens at Yew Tree Farm, Coniston, are enjoying seeds that have fallen from a bale of hay harvested from the nearby fields.

Above them a lath and plaster wall forms the end of a spinning gallery, for which this barn is famed. These galleries, cantilevered platforms at first floor level, are unique to the Lake District. They support the roof above them by means of wooden uprights and they

have a most pleasing appearance. Due to the unfavourable climate it is probable that they were used to dry flax hemp and wool rather than for spinning, or even simply as covered access to the stores.

From a scene such as this, where farming is run on traditional lines, it is easy to imagine a rural idyll. Though the farming calendar remains the same, big contractors now bale the hay.

Lime Kiln
LEVENS NEAR KENDAL

These simple buildings were used for the straightforward task of turning limestone into quicklime. Lime sweetens the land by reducing acidity. It is also the basis for traditional mortar, plaster and renders. Early attempts at burning limestone took place in small depressions on hillsides. A primitive oven was made by igniting the limestone and covering it with clay and turf. From these small beginnings the kiln developed.

Large landowners, groups of farmers or individuals produced lime for their own use. Kilns were usually sited by a quarry. They were built into hillsides whenever possible so that they could be 'top loaded'; if not a ramp was constructed. Small pieces of newly quarried limestone were layered with available fuel, such as wood, peat charcoal or, later on, coal. The opening at the base of the kiln was a combined fire-and-draw hole. After burning for a day or two the lime was drawn off for use.

Old Quarry
HODGE CLOSE CONISTON

Hodge Close quarry is over 92 metres deep. The bedding of the light green slate is almost vertical so the open head quarry had to be dug deep, causing unavoidable extraction problems. Slate commanded a good price, but extraction was costly so it was not the availability which determined whether a quarry was worked. Flooding was always a danger. There was much pumping and an arrangement to take away the surface spring water.

This quarry started life in the 1780s and closed in 1964. As the quarry deepened, devices had to be found to lift and move the slate to places where it could be worked. At various times a water balance lift, a steam crane and a Blondin aerial crane (named after the famous tightrope walker), were used. The latter was suspended over the quarry on a steel cable.

Maintenance of the quarry face was essential as blocks could detach themselves and present an enormous danger. Exposed to the elements, such faces became unstable. At Hodge Close in 1885 over 1000 tons of rock fell into the pit. Five years later the steam crane shared the same fate.

Winter Feeding
NEAR KENDAL

Snow comes to the fells in November, first in falls that often disappear quickly and later to stay on the highest peaks, often till early spring. The leaden skies threaten a further snowfall as the sheep enjoy the sweet hay, which holds a memory of warmer times.

These sheep, Kendal Rough Fell sheep, are fortunate for their long dense coats shrug off the rain and snow. Their name aptly describes their habitation and they thrive where other breeds would not survive. They are not situated as inaccessibly here as some of their less fortunate relatives who have to wait for the tractor to climb the

slopes and the farmer to toss down the hay bales. Their first winter is spent away from the hills but, once mature, sheep are hardy creatures. Only when there are heavy snowfalls will the farmer take his dogs and guide the flock down the slopes.

Fell sheep such as these lamb late in the season when the weather is kinder to their offspring. When they are shorn later, their is wool usually made into warm carpets.

Arched Hogg Hole
LICKLE VALLEY

Hoggs are yearling sheep. In order to allow them to move freely for grazing, openings are made in walls. The simplest way of making an opening is to place a flat rock across a gap in the wall and build above it, but wallers are proud of their skills and devise more impressive ways to achieve this. As a result, many walls deserve close observation, as they bear excellent witness to man's ingenuity. In the Lickle Valley, a highly skilled waller built this Hogg hole, and there are many other examples of gable-shaped entrances.

The farmer could also use these holes for other purposes, for example, he could 'drive' a hogg through to be captured, then close it with a large stone. A similar construction was a 'rabbit snoop'. This was a small

opening through which a rabbit could pass. A counterweighted trapdoor, set in a wooden trough and leading to a stone-lined pit on the other side, consigned the rabbit to await collection.

Sometimes post boxes are incorporated in a roadside wall. Other features to be seen are stone gateposts, which have opposite rows of holes, so that poles could be laid across instead of a gate. If a wall has a clearly defined vertical join, this signifies that responsibility for upkeep of the wall has changed.

Kendal Rough Fell Sheep
HOWGILL FELLS LUNE VALLEY

These Kendal Rough Fell sheep have benefited from living at a reasonably low altitude. Their healthy lambs look strong and active and each ewe has twins.

Behind are the Howgill Fells. They are east of Central Lakeland with smooth contours and no trees to clothe their slopes. Remnants of the winter snows can be seen where shadows linger and gullies fall.

The railway viaduct straddling the valley was built by the London and North West Railway Company. The intention was to build a new main line to West Yorkshire and Scotland. The Beck Foot Viaduct, better known as the Lowgill Viaduct, was part of the scheme. Political wrangling led to the building of the Settle to Carlisle line, reducing its predecessor to a mere branch line. It carried passengers until 1954 and special trains were put on to transport boys from boarding school at Sedbergh at end of term. It continued to carry freight until 1966, when it finally closed. The area was not, however, left without transport as the main line to Scotland is not far. The M6 motorway was constructed in the late 1960s.

Guiding Walls
LICKLE VALLEY NEAR BROUGHTON-IN-FURNESS

Seeing walls stretching across or down a fellside or neatly enclosing a field, makes one marvel at the skill of the waller and sometimes question why a wall is situated in such a remote or difficult place.

Fell farmers often own hundreds or thousands of sheep which, at various times of year, need to be collected from the fell. There is often no need to take the animals down to the farm because pens are often conveniently placed lower on the fellside.

The shepherd and his dogs drive the sheep off the fells to a natural collecting point – often a valley head. From there they are herded through the widely spaced walls called 'out gangs' which funnel the sheep in a steady stream between two parallel walls to the pens. The rough track between walls such as these is designed to guide and control the flow of traffic.

'Out gangs' assist the farmer and walls can help in other ways too: they offer shelter to the sheep, and prevent them from wandering on to or over cliffs where they may perish or become 'crag fast'. In such locations a waller has to maintain a horizontal layering of the wall, otherwise it will, eventually, slide down the hillside.

Jersey Cow
LYNDALE

Most people like to imagine the milk they drink comes from a beautiful Jersey cow living in a field of buttercups. Once they taste the thick, creamy, delicious milk they may then refuse to drink any more of the thin, bluish, skimmed varieties. Production for modern markets, however, is a balance and the farmer has to produce what the market demands. Jersey cows produce milk for a 'niche market', a small fawn oasis surrounded by a desert of black and white cattle.

This contented cow lives on a small, mixed agricultural enterprise where profit is not everything, and the milk is consumed, unpasturized, by the family running the enterprise. The land was once part of a wide valley across which the River Winster roamed on its way to Morecambe Bay. Now it is canalized and the land drained. The rich silt grows lush crops of wild flowers and grasses, when not sown with rye grass.

Raised on organically farmed meadows, unstressed by the need to produce the maximum amount of milk possible for her breed, she is, indeed, a happy cow.

Boat Landings
BUTTERMERE

Great demands are made upon the Lake District and it would be impossible to preserve the beauty of the area at the same time as satisfying every economic and recreational demand.

The National Trust owns Buttermere Lake and most of the valley. It also controls the majority of what remains of the valley by means of restrictive covenants. There is much to be protected. The valley sides sweep down to the small meadows. There are waterfalls and crags above which buzzards and peregrines fly; there are deer in the forest, all bathed in peace and solitude.

Once there were thriving slate quarries at Honister, and wool was carded and spun, but now tourism is the major source of income. The holiday season has lengthened as more people visit throughout the year. Campsites and youth hostels accommodate educational groups, providing activities such as fishing, walking and rock climbing. As well as boats and cottages for hire, there is a wide range of hotels and guest houses, with many farmers' wives offering bed and breakfast for visitors. Hill farming still flourishes, with many farmers keeping the hardy Herdwick breed of sheep.

Despite the growth in tourism, peace and tranquillity can still be found by those prepared to put on their walking boots and venture a little way.

Wind Farm
KIRKBY-IN-FURNESS

A wind turbine is undoubtedly modern. Usually it is white, standing 25 to 30 metres high with two or three blades rotating and reflecting the sunlight.

These structures are not beneficial to the views of Lakeland fells and dales and at present they are excluded from areas of great beauty. This policy does not banish them from every hillside, however; they stand against the skyline at Kirby Moor in South West Lakeland above the village of Grizebeck.

There are 12 turbines providing energy sufficient for 4000 homes. National Wind Power re-landscaped the area to how it was before, once the cables had been hand-laid. The siting of such farms is a contentious issue, many are found lower down on the coastal plains and by the sea in, as yet, small numbers. It is estimated by the year 2025 wind energy nationally could contribute as much as 20 per cent of total energy requirements.

To reduce pollution of our atmosphere without visually polluting our landscape makes siting future farms at sea an attractive possibility.

Cultivated Land
DUDDON VALLEY

Flatter land on valley bottoms is precious and, once cleared of stones, these areas often became the winter larder for the farmers and their animals. At first land was cultivated in small plots, or strips, on a communal basis, but with time each farm acquired its own fields. Animals were excluded from new fields by a wall known as a ring garth and only allowed to graze in them between late autumn and spring.

These fields in the Duddon Valley were farmed on a yearly rotation of oats, potatoes, kale or turnips and then oats and grass sown together. Once the oats were harvested, the grass grew taller and hay was made. For the following five or six years some remained as hayfields, allowing the soil to regenerate itself. The oats and potatoes were for the farmer and his family, the roots and hay for the livestock. Ewes were brought here for lambing, and later for mating.

Now you will find grazing cattle, or grass instead of hay. The fields are still important for lambing and tupping time, but crops grown here are no longer the farmer's only source of food.

Remains of a Head Race
CONISTON FELLS

One of the main problems associated with deep mining is the accumulation of groundwater and the subsequent risk of flooding. Ironically, as water was being pumped out at lower levels, waterwheels were erected close to the top of the shafts of the Coniston Copper Mines. Deep ditches called leats were dug, contouring along the hills, with branches to feed and collect water from the waterwheels they served.

Levers Water, a tarn standing above many of the shafts, was of great importance to the design, as were natural watercourses such as Red Dell Beck. In 1682 work was carried out to repair the dam at Levers Water damaged during the Civil War. The area around the tarn was already mined to the shoreline. So great were the demands for water that a decision was made to secure these workings and raise the waterlevel.

There were many large waterwheels raising ore from the mines. One example, installed in 1852, measured 13.5 metres in diameter. Waterpower was also needed to work pumps and stamping mills and to wash the ore.

Leats can be traced when the sun is shining for they cast shadows; on duller days changes to the vegetation reveal their routes.

Potash Pit
LICKLE VALLEY NEAR BROUGHTON-IN-FURNESS

The Lake District has produced wool for centuries. Sheep are practically the only animals that tolerate the climatic conditions and the harshness of the landscape.

Woollen cloth was produced in large quantity and exported to other areas, but it was often coarse and loosely woven, and needed felting. To bind the fibres together, the cloth went to fulling mills, where it was soaked in soft brown soapy water and beaten with trip hammers. The soap had to be manufactured and for that potash was required. A pit of stone was constructed and a large cauldron of copper strips was made to fit inside. Underneath a tunnel fireplace was fuelled and birch twigs or bracken burnt to ashes. When cooled, lime and water were added and

the mixture was then boiled with tallow to produce soft soap.

Potash pits are located close to sources of raw material and where they can easily be top loaded. Bracken-covered hillsides with woods nearby were ideal.

Peat-cutting Tools
LEVENS NEAR KENDAL

When peat is first cut, it is placed on a spreading ground where, by being placed on its side, much of the water held in the peat drains away into the earth. Only when its outer surface is dry and crusty can peat be moved; otherwise it would fall apart. Peat does not need heavy tools to work it, but the supporting tools do need to be sharp-edged.

Because it is cut in 20-metre-wide strips, the face recedes as it is cut, and if the adjoining strip is not  cut back at the same rate, this would make it difficult to work the sides. The two cutting tools each have a sharpened edge and are designed so that one can cut and lift from the left and from the right.

Initially the top covering of the peat is removed with a tom spade. When the peat is revealed, it is cut horizontally. The worker stands in front of the face and slides the sharp blade in to cut the required depth of peat. A quick flick tears the other edge of the peat, then the sodds are taken off for drying. After further drying in stacks, in an airy hut, the sods are ready for the fire.

Shepherd
CRINKLE CRAGS GREAT LANGDALE

A shepherd gathers his flock many times throughout the year. Sometimes his tasks can be accomplished in gathering pens sited on the hillside, but if not, the sheep are returned to the farm.

In early spring the ewes are brought down to spend time on the intake pasture, close to the farm, in preparation for lambing. Lambing is a stressful time, with orphaned lambs and bereaved ewes resisting the best efforts of the shepherd get the job done. There are difficult births to deal with, and some lambs fail to live. When the lambs are older they have their ears clipped to denote ownership. Each lamb is dosed for fluke, tups are castrated and tails docked. At dipping time there is much heavy and closely regulated work to be done. Similarly, clipping time is also a period of great activity, after which the sheep need little encouragement to return to the peace of the fell.

In the past, throughout summer and into autumn, a series of shows and shepherds' meets were held on hillsides, where stray sheep and news were exchanged. These days sports and amusements are on offer too, and the meets are usually held near a local hostelry.

The hound pictured here is a trail hound to whom this walk on the fells is a mere stroll.

Marking the Tup
LITTLE LANGDALE

Farming is based on renewal: each year young animals must be raised and new crops grown for the farm to thrive.

In order to ensure this, a calendar of events has evolved for the farming year. On the Little Langdale National Trust farm, George Birkett's sheep are mated in time to produce lambs in the second half of April, when the grass starts to grow. Swaledale ewes are strong. Multiple births are viewed as less important than off-spring that thrive.

Hill sheep are hardy creatures, but a farmer should not stress them unduly. A lowland farmer can mate his sheep in their second year. George has to wait for them to mature a further year before introducing them to the tup. Tup is this area's name for a ram, and November is 'tupping time'. There are thirty tups kept on Birk Howe Farm and each can serve between fifty and sixty ewes. They need to be in good condition, so they graze the better grass low down. The ewes seen here are being gathered off the fellside where they have spent the summer.

By putting different coloured dye on the bellies of the tups, called 'redding', George can follow the progress of each ram and see which ewe is mated. The lambs will also be monitored and progeny of the best tups kept for future years.

Stony Hazel Forge
RUSLAND VALLEY

In 1718 the site of Stony Hazel Forge was leased by Rowland Taylor for the building of 'a Bloomery Forge, Coalhouse, Dam and other Appurtenances necessary for the said works'. He was allowed to cut down and carry away all wood growing above the works but this was scarcely enough as iron production needed copious amounts of charcoal.

A bloomery produced low-grade iron. Local hematite ore was heated with charcoal in a small bowl-shaped hearth. Air was introduced by bellows and the ore melted down. The temperatures achieved were too low to allow the iron to run freely, so the slag left behind produced a pasty lump. Water from the dam flowed down a head race on to a waterwheel which powered a hammer. The lump was consolidated by repeated blows by the hammer.

This process was already outdated when the bloomery was built. In the first years of operation there were several disastrous fires, followed by reconstruction and a few productive years. Finally the lease was bought by two larger and more 'modern' producers who took out the equipment and allowed the buildings to decay. Some evidence of the forge remains in this delightful woodland, the largest of which housed the hearth.

Backbarrow Iron Works
LEVEN VALLEY NEAR WINDERMERE

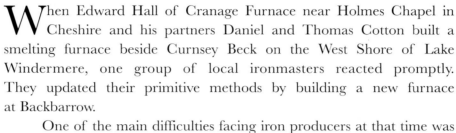

When Edward Hall of Cranage Furnace near Holmes Chapel in Cheshire and his partners Daniel and Thomas Cotton built a smelting furnace beside Curnsey Beck on the West Shore of Lake Windermere, one group of local ironmasters reacted promptly. They updated their primitive methods by building a new furnace at Backbarrow.

One of the main difficulties facing iron producers at that time was obtaining charcoal and the two companies soon realized that to compete would only raise the price of fuel. In 1712, only one year after setting up their furnaces, they entered a price-fixing agreement. This was a close relationship which continued and spread to the management of prices for all furnace requirements.

The partnership at Backbarrow was mainly Quaker in origin. Through marriage and kinship they had connections in Bristol and the surrounding area. Abraham Derby I was one such contact and one relative became a partner in the Coalbrookdale Iron Works.

Furnaces such as these, though locally important, never produced large amounts of iron and the Curnsey furnace was demolished in 1750. Backbarrow continued and was able to withstand competition from new coke-fluid furnaces elsewhere because of a specialized section of the market that required hematite pig iron. Charcoal was last used at Backbarrow in 1926, after which the works converted to coke.

The increasing competition from modern plants finally caused Backbarrow's closure in the 1960s.

Newly Laid Hedge
NEAR NEWBY BRIDGE WINDERMERE

It is not advisable to lay a hedge when very cold weather is expected because frost can damage or even kill the newly cut hedge. When you see the depth of the cut it becomes easy to understand this fact and difficult to believe that a hedge can take such butchery and survive under normal circumstances.

Before laying, a hedge should have grown and produced many upright stems. Hawthorn and blackthorn are best, but oak, ash and hazel can also be left if gaps need to be filled. Some stock like to nibble the oak, ash and hazel, however. Once October arrives and the sap is no longer rising the hedger can clear and select his plants. A deep incision is made in the remaining growth as close to the ground as possible. This growth is then bent and woven, all the while being pressed down and guided by stakes.

Traditionally a billhook was used, but now chainsaws can do much of the initial thinning. A final trimming with a long hook gives a good finish and sometimes a strand of barbed wire is included to deter livestock.

Over 1000 years ago parish registers were documenting hedgerows and since that time they have enriched our countryside by perpetuating ancient skills.

Flag Wall
NEAR HAWKSHEAD

Flag quarries produced, as their name suggests, large pieces of flat rock of suitable width for walls, floors, roofs and other building tasks. At Hawkshead they are used to support a first floor jettied gable, and in Ambleside for balustrades on galleries. This wall of slate is known as a shard fence, and is one of many found south of the village of Hawkshead, just north of the Youth Hostel.

The sedimentary slates used here come from a bed that runs across the central Lake District, along a limestone fault line. The quarry was situated above the River Brathay and the slates are known as Brathay flags, but there are other quarries such as those at Coniston. Because the source of suitable material is limited, such walls are seen in some areas only.

As sheep are notorious for climbing and jumping, these fences have many advantages. They are set to interlock so that stock cannot squeeze through and they offer no foothold or platform from which to jump. When set deeply in the ground they are not easily moved and they make good field boundaries.

The lichens that thrive on these slates provide interesting colour and texture in the ever-changing light, and are an added bonus.

Blackthorn Hedge
WINSTER VALLEY

Blackthorn makes a wonderful hedge. It is native to our landscape and flowers profusely in spring, but its pretty appearance masks the long, hard sharp spines that erupt from its stems. No man or beast enjoys contact with this plant so it makes an ideal stock-proof barrier. As a source of food for wildlife, a hedge such as this is limited, but it is planted to do a job and few sheep would contemplate a close encounter.

At its base animals and plants use it as a byway along which to travel, tentatively spreading outwards from an adjoining wood or headland to colonize new areas. Bats often follow hedges and birds shelter from predators within fortified nesting sites.

When the flowers are shed the leaves appear and with approaching autumn the wild blackthorn will offer small hazy purple fruits known as sloes. Mixed with gin and sugar and left to mature, they produce delicious sloe gin, a traditional accompaniment to rural Christmas festivities.

Swirl How and Great Carrs
LITTLE LANGDALE

Fell Foot is an apt name for this working sheep farm. Down in the valley, surrounded by good pasture, it also formerly served as a place of rest and refreshment for the traveller.

Nearby, the Roman road from the fort at Galava, Ambleside begins the ascent of Wrynose Pass, then visits the Duddon and Eskdale valleys before finally reaching the coast at the port of Ravensglass.

Later Norsemen built a 'thingmound' here, a terraced hillock where settlers met to iron out disputes and possibly make decisions concerning the government of the Langdale valleys.

It is not known how long there has been a building on this site, but it was documented as a grand house in 1670 and there are indications that the north wing is of sixteenth-century construction. There are tales of smuggling both in and out of the valleys and Fell Foot, a good distance away from other habitation, was well placed for secret meetings. Smugglers may no longer find a welcome but accommodation is still provided.

Old Quarry and Mine
CONISTON

Four hundred and fifty million years ago the huge volcanoes that were active in this region spewed out the dust and ash that forms the slate which so much a part of this tranquil scene.

Beneath the path is the waste, the by-product of slate quarrying, an activity with ancient origins. This wonderful material was known to the Romans who used it to roof their fort at Watercrook.

Seen through the trees, the quarry face belies its danger. Rock falls are the enemy of the quarryman and the face is not to be trusted. The quarry started its life as a closed head quarry with men working the seam at various levels. Then the roof was removed to give access from above, a very dangerous development. In an open head quarry, men worked in all weathers, six days a week, for meagre wages. They laboured hard and drank hard; there were times of depression and riot, but close ties, loyalties and team spirit made for strong communities.

Copper Mines
CONISTON

The entrance to Gaunts Level is most attractive and draws the eye inwards and onwards to explore the tunnel beyond. This tunnel is blocked after 97 metres and should be investigated with great caution. Other such temptations to explore are to be avoided as old tunnels can be extremely dangerous.

Mining began at Coniston Copper Mines in about 1600 when German workers were brought to the area by the Elizabethan Company of Mines Royal. Due to their hard work the veins had been mined to a depth of 61 metres at the outbreak of the Civil War. The destruction of smelters at Keswick caused production to cease. This state of affairs did not last long and there were a succession of proprietors who developed the mines, which reached peak production in the nineteenth century when much copper was needed to sheath the hulls of wooden sailing ships.

Tunnels were driven into the mountain sides to connect with the deepening working of the vein. They made the extraction of the ore easier as it no longer had to be raised to the top of the shaft. They could also be used to draw water away from the mine to streams or channels which carried it away down the hillside.

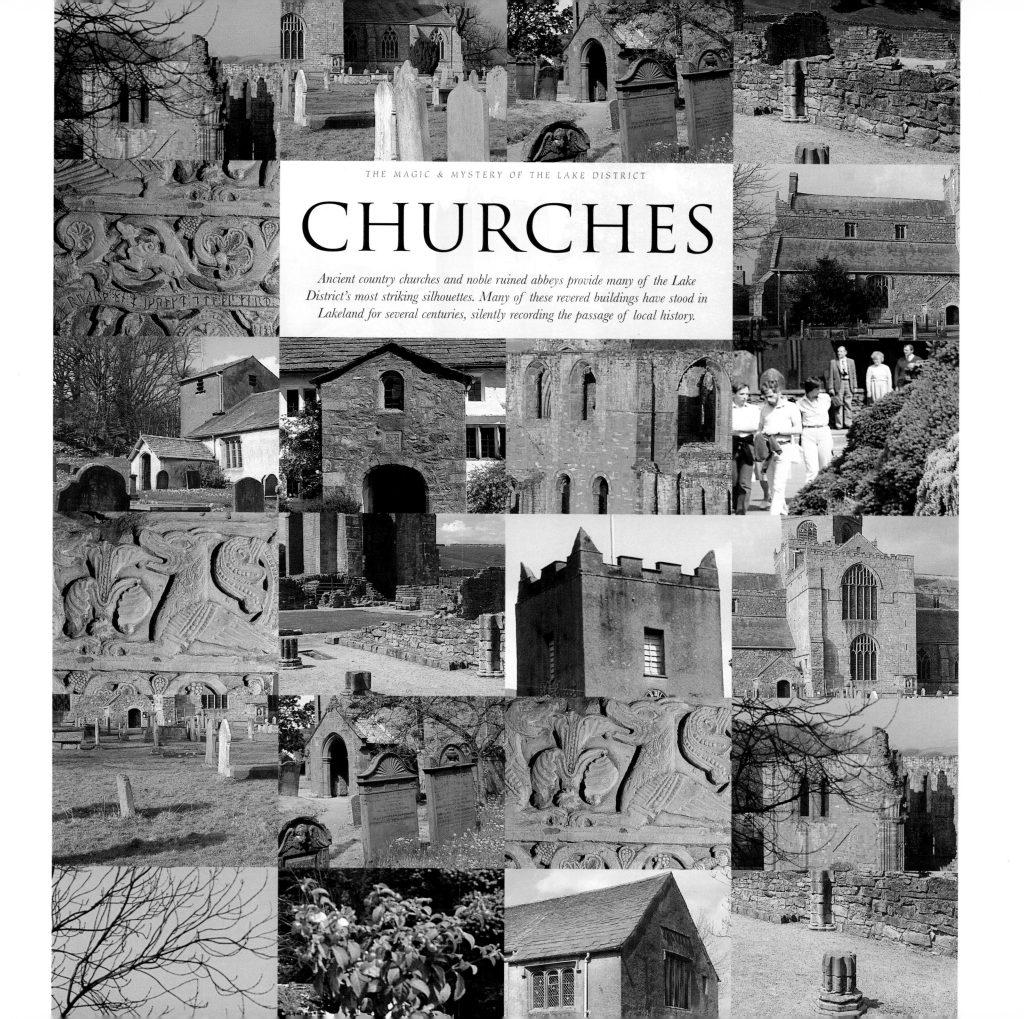

CHURCHES

Ancient country churches and noble ruined abbeys provide many of the Lake District's most striking silhouettes. Many of these revered buildings have stood in Lakeland for several centuries, silently recording the passage of local history.

St Oswald's Church
GRASMERE

Grasmere's tranquil church is a mecca for tourists and lovers of literature from all over the world. The ancient church, set amidst verdant scenery, is the final resting place of the poet William Wordsworth, along with his sister Dorothy and other family members. Wordsworth lived from 1770 until 1850. He is Britain's most-read Romantic poet, achieving great fame in his lifetime and being made Poet Laureate in 1843. Despite his fame, Wordsworth chose to remain in his beloved Lake District, drawing inspiration from the marvellous scenery around his home. Within St Oswald's church is a commemorative carving, created by Thomas Woolner, honouring the life of William Wordsworth.

...A Power is passing from the earth
To breathless Nature's dark abyss;
But when the great and good depart
What is it more than this –

That Man, who is from God sent forth
Doth yet again to God return? –
Such ebb and flow must ever be,
Then wherefore should we mourn?

William Wordsworth,
'Lines Composed at Grasmere'

Quaker Meeting House
BRIGG FLATTS NEAR KIRKBY LONSDALE

The Quaker movement was founded by an English lay preacher, George Fox (1624–1691), some time around 1647. The correct name for this Christian community is the Society of Friends, but they have been known by the name of Quakers almost since their inception. The nickname derives from the belief that the worshipping congregation 'quake' in the awesome presence of God.

The Society of Friends is a pacific community, staunchly opposed to war and adhering strongly to the words of the scriptures. Many Friends emigrated to America in the seventeenth century and were amongst the first to oppose slavery (with their official protests dating back to as long ago as 1688) and the harsh treatment of the Native Americans.

The Lake District was a natural place for the peace-loving Friends to live. The region has early associations with the Society – there is a rock on Firbank Fell known as 'Fox's Pulpit' from which George Fox preached a three-hour sermon to a large congregation.

Viking Cross
GOSFORTH

The mountains that make up so much of the Lake District were a useful deterrent to many would-be invaders and Lakeland remained undisturbed for several centuries after the Roman conquest. It was not until some time around the tenth century that new invaders started to arrive, warriors from Scandinavia for whom the climate and countryside of the Lake District seemed like a home from home.

This Viking cross, created by settlers from Denmark, dates from the late tenth century. It is an elegant reminder of a culture that shaped so much of the Lake District's history. Many names in the surrounding area come from the ancient Norse language: the word 'fell' comes from the Norse word 'fiall' meaning mountain, and the word 'pen' (as in the Pennines) means 'hill'.

Gosforth's cross is almost 4.5 metres high and is renowned as an exceptional example of Anglo-Norse collaboration. The carved scenes that appear on the cross are among the earliest known depictions of Viking-Christian mythology.

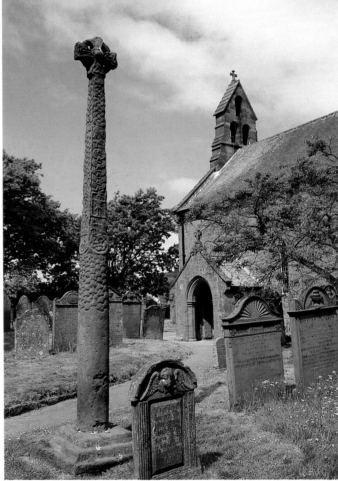

Cartmel Fell Church
CARTMEL

Cartmel Fell Church dates back to the early part of the sixteenth century. It was built for the people living in the areas surrounding Cartmel, but who lived too far away to attend the services held at Cartmel Priory. The church is sited roughly seven miles from the village itself.

In medieval times, Cartmel Fell Priory was a welcoming Christian haven in which local people could sit and contemplate or kneel and pray

– a gentle contrast to the many high church, Godfearing edifices built around the same time. The interior of the church remains carefully tended to this day and features some of the district's most splendid examples of wood artistry.

The area around Cartmel is renowned for its variety of wildlife and the beauty of its countryside. The town of Cartmel has at its centre an ancient market square, and the buildings have changed little since the inn was used as a coaching house.

Cartmel Priory
CARTMEL

The majestic Priory Church of St Mary and St Michael which stands at the heart of Cartmel's market square dates back over 800 years. In 1188, building work began on a church at this site and since then a great deal of later architecture has grown up around the twelfth-century stones. The completion of the priory gave its small village a new importance in twelfth-century England. Despite its small size – Cartmel originally comprised just 22 acres – Cartmel Priory became the central part of a large parish stretching from Ulverston to Windermere and Beetham.

The central tower of this elegant church is perhaps its most outstanding feature – noteworthy because of its peculiar shape. In keeping with most churches of its time, it is square but, unusually, it stands at a diagonal angle.

Expansive Gothic windows flood the church's interior with a wealth of natural light, lustrously bathing the well-worn gravestones that pave the floor. Several of these indoor tombs house the bones of those who were drowned many centuries ago. In years past, one could walk across Morecambe Bay at low tide and all too often unfortunates, unaware of the quick change in tides, were swept to their death.

Furness Abbey
NEAR BARROW-IN-FURNESS

Here, where, of havoc tired and rash undoing,
Man left this Structure to become Time's prey,
A soothing spirit follows in the way
That Nature takes...

William Wordsworth, 'At Furness Abbey'

The ruins of this impressive abbey have witnessed a long, rich and chequered history. Monks of the order of Savigny began to build their place of worship, on this site, as long ago as 1127. It has remained a holy place ever since. The fruits of the monks' labour eventually passed to a Cistercian community – for a time England's richest and most influential religious order. Under the Cistercians, Furness Abbey became one of the country's most wealthy religious communities and the owner of land in present-day Cumbria, Ireland and the Isle of Man.

The abbey was built in what has become known as the Vale of Deadly Nightshade, a lushly wooded area dense with *Bella donna*. This rich, green valley still surrounds the tremendous ruins, providing the perfect backdrop to the sun-warmed red sandstone.

The location of Furness has proved a somewhat unfortunate one. Twice the abbey was attacked by invaders from Scotland, although it was England's own king, Henry VIII, who finally sealed the abbey's fate. Much of the building was razed to the ground when it gained the dubious distinction of being the first of Britain's abbeys to suffer Dissolution.

Shap Abbey
NEAR PENRITH

After eight centuries of turbulence, Shap's enormous abbey is a desolate ruin, the only part of its structure that remains relatively intact is its sixteenth-century tower. Many of the abbey's original stones were purloined for use on the nearby Lowther Castle. The foundations of the abbey date back to the twelfth century – building work first began on an abbey on this site in 1180.

In 1199 a community of Premonstratensian canons took up residence in Shap Abbey. The Premonstratensian movement was begun in France by Canon, later St, Norbert. He founded the movement in 1120 at Prémontré near Laon in France. It was an order exclusively for canons – those who were between monks and friars in the religious hierarchy.

St Norbert came from a noble German family whose property was in the Rhineland. Until the age of 35 he led a typical nobleman's life, serving as a courtier in the royal house. After a near-death experience he underwent a similar conversion to that of St Paul on the road to Damascus and, renouncing all his worldly goods to raise money for the poor, became a religious zealot, travelling widely in his native Germany and through other parts of Europe, most notably France and Italy.

Font at Bridekirk Church
NEAR COCKERMOUTH

The font at Bridekirk church dates back to the mid-twelfth century. It is a marvellous piece of stonemasonry, lavishly decorated with figures, plants and animals. A font is always positioned near the church door as baptism marks the entrance of a child to the Christian church and the water in the font is used to mark the child's head with the sign of the cross.

This region, although best known as the birthplace of William Wordsworth, has many other fascinating historical associations. Just six years before the birth of the poet, the famous mutineer, Fletcher Christian was born in a small rural area near here known as Moorland Close.

Cockermouth was created a market town by Royal Charter in 1221, and since that time has been a vibrant community and an important part of Lake District life. The town has a twelfth-century castle, built to protect the region from Scottish attacks; it was also used by Oliver Cromwell's soldiers during the English Civil War of the mid-seventeenth century. Cockermouth is also the site of Workington Hall, one of the places Mary, Queen of Scots, stayed in en route from Scotland to England. It was, in fact, where she enjoyed her very last night of freedom.

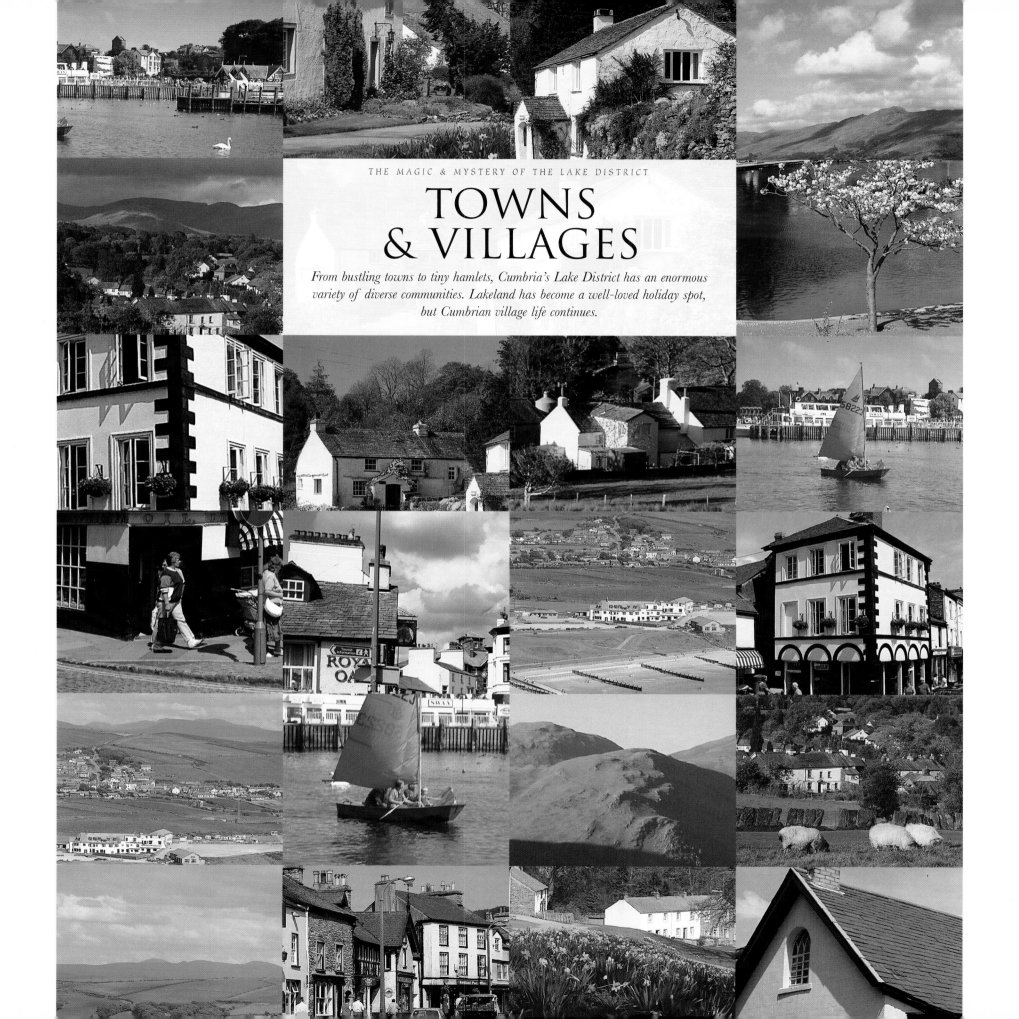

TOWNS & VILLAGES

From bustling towns to tiny hamlets, Cumbria's Lake District has an enormous variety of diverse communities. Lakeland has become a well-loved holiday spot, but Cumbrian village life continues.

Askham
NEAR PENRITH

One of the prettiest villages in the Lake District is Askham, a small community sited not far from Penrith. The village has a shape similar to that of a rugby ball with seventeenth-century houses curving around the edges. The main road through the village is flanked by wide greens, which are a riot of colour in spring. There are two pubs in the village, but the village school closed down and children now have to go to a nearby town for their schooling.

Just outside Askham is the family home of the Earls of Lonsdale, the estate of Lowther which includes Lowther Castle. The Castle, constructed under the guidance of Sir Robert Smirke, an eminent architect, dates back to around 1810. The then Earl of Lonsdale for whom it was built was the patron of William Wordsworth and a popular local figure.

View to the Town
HAWKSHEAD

Hawkshead is a tiny village with a population of roughly 700. It lies to the south of Ambleside and to the left of the magnificent Lake Windermere at an altitude of 228 metres above sea level. In the eleventh and twelfth centuries, Hawkshead was a major centre of Lakeland industry, producing large quantities of wool, a commodity much in demand by those who had to endure the rigours of a Lake District winter. Most of the buildings, however, date back only as far as the seventeenth century – picturesque houses and shops set in cobbled yards, all with carefully tended gardens. There is also the grammar school, attended by William Wordsworth between 1779 and 1787, and the old Hawkshead courthouse.

The town is also strongly associated with Beatrix Potter. In the building formerly used as a solicitor's office by her husband, William Heelis, there is a gallery dedicated to the great writer and illustrator, displaying many fine examples of her work.

A Kendal Street
KENDAL

The world-famous market town of Kendal is the largest town in the Lake District with a population of about 25,000. It is often called the Gateway to the Lakes and has been attracting visitors for centuries. At the top of Castle Hill is the ruined Kendal Castle, once the home of the Parr family. They are buried in their family vault in Kendal Parish Church. Both the castle and church date back to the thirteenth century.

Kendal has long been a centre for industry. In the past, thriving cottage industries specialized in traditional crafts and today many still survive alongside more modern industries and tourism. The town's name has been made famous by two of its creations: a distinctive yellow woollen material, popular in centuries past and misleadingly named Kendal Green – it is mentioned in Shakespeare's play *Henry V*; the other is the town's most famous export, Kendal Mintcake – a high-energy, incredibly sweet bar, made mainly from sugar and peppermint oil, and much valued by mountain climbers and long-distance hikers. Kendal Mintcake is reputed to have been taken to the summits of almost all the world's conquered mountains.

Springtime View
GRANGE-OVER-SANDS

The name of this little Cumbrian town comes from its earliest occupation, that of a granary for a nearby monastic community. For many centuries, Grange-over-Sands was a small little-known community. All this changed in 1857 when it became part of England's fast-growing railway network. By the end of the Victorian era, and throughout the Edwardian age, Grange-over-Sands was a highly popular and fashionable seaside resort. The ornamental gardens and peaceful promenade date from that period.

Before the advent of the railway, there was a regular stage coach that ran from Lancaster to Ulverston, stopping en route at Grange-over-Sands. To ensure that travellers attained safe passage over the muddy sands of Morecambe Bay, a guide was appointed, paid for by the Duchy of Lancaster on behalf of the Queen. Today there is still a Queen's guide, though now only over the summer months, to help tourists find their way across what can be a treacherous route. The appointed guide is always a fisherman as he has to know Morecambe's capricious tides intimately.

Buttermere Village
BUTTERMERE

The bewitching Lakeland valley of Buttermere is reached via a small winding road through the Derwent Fells. Once at the village, set amid verdant slopes, walkers can take one of the Lake District's most well-trodden routes, a gentle path around the outside seam of Buttermere's lake.

The word Buttermere, meaning 'dairy pasture lake', pays tribute to the district's long history of agricultural excellence. Several centuries ago, the lake at Buttermere was part of the neighbouring Crunnock Water, but excess silt in the water built up to form a strip of land dividing the two.

In the village of Buttermere stands a small, ancient church that contains a memorial plaque to Alfred Wainwright. Wainwright was a tireless walker of the Lakeland region and, from the 1950s onwards, he compiled the records of his walks in the area. His personal accounts were exquisitely hand-written and illustrated, and turned into a book entitled *Pictorial Guides*. To this day there is no better guide to the district for walkers than Alfred Wainwright's lovingly fashioned masterpiece.

Lake Road
AMBLESIDE

Lake Road takes tourists and travellers from the head of Lake Windermere at Waterhead into the busy tourist centre of Ambleside, where they may stay in one of the numerous hotels or guest houses, or travel on into the Central Lakes on one of the ancient routes.

Ambleside has always been a busy place, even before the rise in tourism. There were many mills, including bobbin mills, corn mills, fulling mills, bark mills and even cotton and paper mills. When a railhead opened in Windermere in 1847, Ambleside became more accessible to the general public, who having read of Lakeland's charms in the work of Romantic poets and writers, visited in droves.

Windermere and Bowness developed more quickly because they were close to the railway. At Ambleside visitors tended to stay longer and use it as a base from which to explore the area. The age of the motorcar brought even more people and saw an even greater expansion in accommodation, shops, cafés and restaurants.

Ambleside and Wansfell
FROM LOUGHRIGG

Seen here from Loughrigg are the towns of Ambleside and Wansfell. Ambleside is centrally placed within the Lake District. It was a valued Roman town and a strategic fort. The Roman invaders built a celebrated road, known today as High Street – not because of its central location in a town, as is usually the case, but because of its altitude. High Street was built to link the fort at Ambleside, known as Galava, with the fort of Brocavum at Brougham. The road is 25 miles long (the Roman mile was slightly shorter than the current recognized mile; in Roman measurement it stretched for 27 miles).

High Street was built on a route previously untrodden by humans and rises to a height of 823 metres. Until the eighteenth century, when the Pennine road, Great Dun Fell Road, was built, Lakeland's High Street was the highest road in England.

St Bees

FROM ST BEES HEAD

The village of St Bees, seen here with the Lakeland fells in the background, has been a settlement for many thousands of years and has a superbly rich history.

St Bees is named after St Bega, a ninth- or tenth-century Irish princess. According to legend, St Bega sailed to Lakeland, landing at the spot now known as St Bees, in *c*.900. She left Ireland to escape an arranged marriage to a Norse chieftain. Her courage and strong religious beliefs deeply affected the local people who well-respected the wisdom in her preaching. In the twelfth century a church was built on this site and dedicated jointly to St Mary and St Bega. Its foundations, however, were built on those of an earlier church, possibly dating back to the time of St Bega's arrival in England.

The small village of St Bees also aroused great archaeological excitement in the early 1980s when a preserved body, dating from the Middle Ages, was uncovered during the excavation of a ruined chapel. It is one of the best-preserved medieval bodies ever to have been found in England.

Bowness Bay
WINDERMERE

A picturesque spot on the shore of Lake Windermere, Bowness Bay is a mecca for sail boats, row boats, steamers and all manner of birds – stately swans, greedy gulls and mellow mallards. This peaceful holiday town would have roused fury in a usually placid William Wordsworth, whose greatest fear was the colonization of his beloved Lake District by hordes of uncivilized holidaymakers.

At the height of England's railway fever in 1844, plans were proposed to extend Kendal's existing railway to the outskirts of Bowness. In a passion, Wordsworth wrote to Prime Minister Gladstone and composed an angry sonnet, which was printed in the *Morning Post*. The poem began with the lines:

Is then no nook of English ground secure
From rank assault...?
William Wordsworth

The Poet Laureate's heart-felt objections did not stem the railway line's extension. No doubt, in its time it has fulfilled Wordsworth's worst fears by conveying ... *the whole of Lancashire, and no small part of Yorkshire, pouring in upon us to meet the men of Durham, and the borderers from Cumberland and Northumberland...* to the shores of the glistening Lake Windermere.

Winster Houses
WINSTER

The hamlet of Winster is located near the head of Winster Valley. The valley is roughly 10 miles long and leads down to the River Kent estuary, not far from Grange-over-Sands.

Winster is often overlooked by the many tourists who flock to the Lake District each year. It is off the beaten track and has no lake, and as such is an unspoilt haven of delightful scenery. This picturesque idyll was threatened about three decades ago when the Corporation of Manchester wanted to dam Winster and flood the valley for use as a reservoir. Fortunately fierce local opposition quashed the idea.

Further along the River Winster is Helton Tarn, a vital water source for early iron works, the machinery of which was powered mainly by steam. The first ever iron boat was built here and, reputedly, sunk in Helton Tarn. The iron works also received a huge commission, from the French government, to make the pipes for the entire Paris water system. After the French order had been fulfilled, several pipes were left over – these were used as supports for buildings within the Winster Valley.

Town Centre
ULVERSTON

Ulverston is a charming market town of cobbled streets lined with speckled grey cottages. It was a centre of industry with small cotton mills, leather works and some iron-ore mining. Today Ulverston is home to much bigger, national businesses.

The town of Ulverston has several varied claims to fame: amongst its sons it counts Sir John Barrow (1764–1848), the explorer and naval officer who founded the highly renowned Royal Geographical Society; and the Hollywood comedian, Stan Laurel, of the famous 1920s comedy duo Laurel and Hardy. Both are celebrated: in 1850, Sir John Barrow's memory was honoured by the building of a lighthouse at the top of Hoad Hill, whilst Stan Laurel's life is celebrated in the hugely popular Laurel and Hardy museum in Ulverston's town centre.

The harbour of Ulverston also boasts a famous landmark – a ship canal built by the eminent Scottish designer-architect John Rennie, in 1796. Rennie is perhaps more famous further south for his construction of London's Waterloo Bridge.

THE MAGIC & MYSTERY OF THE LAKE DISTRICT

TRADITIONS & CULTURE

In few other areas of the British Isles do so many crafts and traditions still thrive. The old ritual of rushbearing and the annual Appleby Horse Fair are just two examples of the Lake District's wealth of cultural heritage.

Step and Garland Dancers
KIRKBY LONSDALE

The steps in step and garland dancing were taught to generations of children by dancing masters in villages throughout the Lakes. Any suitable space would do and courses often culminated in a Finishing Ball. Teachers were strict, teaching steps one at a time until each was mastered. A fiddle was played in accompaniment, with the bow also being used to bring the class to order.

At the Finishing Ball the pupils demonstrated their new skills to parents, friends and family. They all had a chance to enjoy themselves at a general dancing session that followed. Dances included the jockey dance, skirt dance, hoop dance, hornpipe and horse-to-Newmarket dance, which were all well-known in the 1700s.

The Step and Garland team was formed twenty-one years ago. Luckily, the steps were still alive in the memories of those who attended classes in their youth and were passed on to the current generation of dancers. Garland dances use hoops or garlands collected from all over the country. The hoops are particularly decorative and present a colourful and enjoyable display.

Christmas
GRANGE-OVER-SANDS

Each December children come with their parents from miles around to celebrate Christmas. Carol singing with the Flookburgh Silver Band is followed by the ceremonial lighting of the Christmas tree by a local dignitary. The tree is claimed to be the tallest living Christmas tree in England and it towers above the Ornamental Gardens in which it stands. The impact of the lights is heightened by their reflection in the waters of the nearby pool and by the wildfowl voicing their approval.

Down the hill from the town centre comes the sound of sleigh bells, with torch bearers leading the way for Father Christmas. Great cheering and excitement follows as he leaves his sledge to take a seat under the canopy outside the gaily decorated shops and cafés. The children who have formed a queue in anticipation of his arrival, become the happy recipients of sweets dispensed by Santa. On the way home there is much contented munching by the children, while parents discuss the relative merits of the competitive shop window displays.

Rushbearing
GRASMERE

The origin of rushbearing is lost in time but as early churches had earth floors, it is probable that it refers to the yearly strewing of these floors with fresh rushes. This ceremony is always on the Saturday following St Oswald's day, 5 August, and the village is filled with onlookers as the participants move in procession around the village. A cross bearer is followed by the choir, then the Bishop of Carlisle leads the main body of the procession with six rush maidens carrying between them a cloth bearing the rushes. Behind them are carried biblical emblems which, together with the rushes, will adorn the church. A band accompanies the walkers to the church for a service after which the more earthly celebrations commence.

Specially made ginger bread, stamped with a cross, is served at a celebration tea following the rushbearing, and this in turn is followed by sport, to bring this festive day to an end. It is a relaxing and happy ending to a day full of tradition and ritual involving the children of the village.

Besoms
SPARK BRIDGE NEAR CONISTON

These witches' brooms are mere bundles of birch twigs cut when the leaves have been shed and before the sap begins to rise, in March. They are stored in barns until summer, when the besom maker begins work at his besom engine. The engine is a device that holds the trimmed 'chats' together whilst the 'spinner' wraps wire around them. A stout ash or hazel pole is then inserted into the head and is firmly beaten home.

A besom sweeps up leaves and twigs, cleans a path, or moves the snow with an efficiency that belies its tattered appearance. Once in use, the ends of the birch split and as the fibres spread, they are able to trap even tiny stones.

Today, besoms are still much in demand with production always struggling a little to keep pace. Those pictured here are for a municipal parks department.

Basket Making

NIBTHWAITE NEAR CONISTON

In former times these elegant but simple baskets were used to harvest potatoes, shovel corn, cast seed and carry bobbins. Their sturdier cousins transported coal and ore in mines and furnaces, a far cry from the log baskets, dried flower containers and garden accessories of today.

The woodlands of South Lakeland are rich in oak, ash and hazel, the raw materials required. The 'swiller' spends much of his time preparing them for use. Young saplings of hazel or ash are steamed and shaped to form the oval rim but the oak demands more attention. It has to be split until only 3 mm thick, then it is smoothed with a draw knife as the swiller sits at his 'mare'. The strips are woven in a set order, each having their end dressed to ensure a firm and tidy attachment to the rim. The subtle colours found in these ribbons of thin oak are produced by the tannin in the water when they are boiled.

'Swill shops' were common, with groups of men and their apprentices working long hours to satisfy demand. The demise of this craft came with the advent of wire baskets. The skill has now almost disappeared. There is little attraction in this hard, laborious work, but maintaining the ancient skills does provide its rewards.

Maypole Dancing
LOWICK FAIR

May Day was a day of 'mad happiness' and a time to celebrate the fertility of the spring. Maypole dancing was an expression of that joy, with much kissing, feasting and playing of games. Recent research claims that maypoles may have been introduced to this country from Scandinavia.

It is thought that the ribbon dance was not introduced until 1836. Prior to this, the most popular dance consisted of two concentric circles, one of girls and one of boys. When a girl stopped opposite a boy, they were meant to kiss. The wantonness of this behaviour caused the Puritans much distress and in consequence many maypoles were felled. However, dancing and celebrations continued and did not decline until the nineteenth century.

Perhaps it was the movement of rural people to the cities, or the competing attractions of theatre and other entertainment, which saw the decline of the maypole dance. By the twentieth century May Day celebrations were a pale shadow of those that had gone before.

Increasing interest in tradition has seen a revival of the May Day celebrations. Local papers are full of pictures of May queens and their attendants at their celebrations.

Market
KENDAL

On Saturdays the 'butter ladies' set out their stalls in Kendal's indoor market. Poultry, butter, eggs and jams, vegetables and cut flowers, lettuce and tomatoes are displayed as they have been for generations. Outside, a few fish stalls in their traditional place and local nurserymen with cut flowers and plants in profusion tempt housewives to part with their money.

Kendalians love their market, as do the inhabitants of surrounding farms and villages whose ancestors came here to sell their agricultural products and handicrafts. This attachment was evident when the right to collect market tolls under the charter of 1198 was purchased by public subscription and then abolished in 1865. An indoor market was also built to commemorate Queen Victoria's Jubilee in 1887. The market stimulated local industry by providing an outlet for locally produced goods. In 1881 the weekly sale of woollen stockings averaged 2,400 pairs.

It has been estimated that Kendal has a catchment area of a 250,000 people, although happily, they do not all visit at once. The markets held on Wednesdays and Saturdays offer a wide range of products and many take the opportunity to browse and buy.

Ice Skating
TARN HOWS

High up between Hawkshead and Coniston, families bring their sledges, skis and skates to enjoy an invigorating day out. Arthur Ransome did just this in 1933 and pictures of that visit are found in *Winter Holiday*.

Each year local residents wait eagerly to see if the tarns will freeze over, for if they do then there is much pleasure to be had from that most traditional winter pastime – skating. Of course there are dangers, but one of the most accessible and beautiful tarns is shallow enough to freeze over quickly. Tarn Hows is extremely pretty, planted with coniferous trees it has many inlets and headlands to delight the eye. The slopes surrounding it present excitement to those who prefer to sledge and many find themselves propelled on to the ice of the tarn, chased by excited dogs and children.

Others find their own peace further from the track. Walkers enjoy the scene soothed by the sun on their face and the gentle swish of the skaters.

Drystone Wallers
DUDDON VALLEY

During the week wallers lived out on the fellside, returning home at weekends. They were poorly paid and often illiterate, but highly skilled – in this respect these National Trust wallers, in the Duddon Valley, resemble them.

The technique of building a wall is little altered from centuries ago, the principle being to construct a long-lasting, well-draining structure that transfers the weight on to the footing stones at its base. Some walls had small quarries nearby, others used stone from field clearance or from rivers. First a shallow trench is prepared and two parallel rows of large footing stones placed on firm foundations. The space between the rows is filled with irregular small stones. These will compact as the wall grows and pressure builds up.

Long cross stones, or throughs, span the width of the wall, binding it together. These are laid at intervals, preventing the wall from bulging and giving lateral strength. A walling frame guides the waller. He pre-determines the shape, and by the use of attached strings, the decreasing width of the wall and its height may be regulated. Cam stones, set on edge, top the wall and deter adventurous sheep.

Horse Fair
APPLEBY

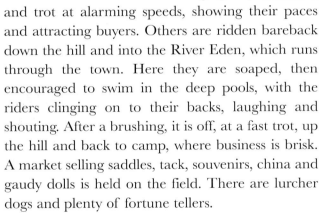

If you have an old gypsy caravan you are proud of, and you want it to be admired by thousands, then Appleby Horse Fair is the place to be. The largest annual gathering of travelling folk in the United Kingdom, the fair has its origins in a charter granted in 1685 by James II. It stated that it was to be conducted on three days in June, the third of which was to be used for the sale of horses.

Generations of old gypsy families are joined by newer traders in their encampment on Fair Hill Field. Lines of horses are tethered to the fences. The road is closed as horses and rigs gallop and trot at alarming speeds, showing their paces and attracting buyers. Others are ridden bareback down the hill and into the River Eden, which runs through the town. Here they are soaped, then encouraged to swim in the deep pools, with the riders clinging on to their backs, laughing and shouting. After a brushing, it is off, at a fast trot, up the hill and back to camp, where business is brisk. A market selling saddles, tack, souvenirs, china and gaudy dolls is held on the field. There are lurcher dogs and plenty of fortune tellers.

After a rowdy exhausting three days, all deals have been done and Appleby resumes its role as a quiet market town.

Mummers Play
BROUGHTON-IN-FURNESS

At Eastertime during the Mummers Play, St George bravely confronts the Prince of Paradise in the square at Broughton-in-Furness. This conflict depicts the end of the old and birth of the new, and is a thinly veiled pre-Christian celebration. The Furness Morris Men who perform it blacken their faces to prevent recognition, which would break the luck associated with the play. The script was written in the nineteenth century, but the Prince is of Moroccan, Minorcan or Turkish origin and dates from the Crusades. He wears paper streamers, which are the oldest form of costuming.

Betty Askett carries a basket and a wooden spoon, a fertility symbol. Tosspot wears his jacket inside out to render him invisible to fairies and evil spirits. Brandishing his sword, St George impresses the audience with tales of his heroic deeds then challenges the Prince. The conflict begins and the Prince soon lies dead. The Doctor has been watching with Little Devil Doubt and rushes on to administer 'Sip Sap', namely rum, to the lifeless Prince. He is soon revived and, like spring, he is reborn.

Weatheriggs Pottery
NEAR PENRITH

The invention of the tile drain brought more land into cultivation and improved pasture. The response of landowners was to encourage the setting up of tile factories and with the abolition of brick tax in 1850, Weatheriggs opened in 1855 at Clifton Dykes south of Penrith, on a seam of red clay. Its future looked bright.

Some years later pottery for domestic use was also produced and the dot, squiggle and dash motif were adopted for decoration. Production had to be fast and no shapes were simple. Between 6000 and 7000 pots were loaded into the beehive kiln for firing. The kiln took six tons of coal and two days to reach the right temperature. Coal was brought in on the Eden Valley Branch line railway, which also took away the finished product.

Earthenware potteries had their ups and downs, being affected by urbanization, changes in methods of cooking, decline in domestic butter and cheese production, economic depression and war. By 1945 there were fewer than a dozen potteries left.

Weatheriggs survived by developing bright innovative home wares and frost-proof garden pots. Tourists were welcomed. In 1973 the pottery was scheduled as an Ancient Monument. Once again its future looks bright.

Charcoal Burning
NEAR BACKBARROW

Plumes of smoke are once more rising from the woods, hinting at an industry slowly returning from the edge of extinction. The power of fire is harnessed, not to consume the smouldering wood but to cause the release of unwanted gases and thus produce charcoal, which burns slowly and produces higher temperatures than wood. During 'charring' the supply of oxygen is strictly controlled, otherwise the wood would simply erupt in flames.

The traditional method of production was to build a carefully graded pitstead or cone of coppiced wood around a central pole. When it was completed, reeds or grass formed a covering and a layer of fine sandy soil closed all the gaps. Lighted charcoal was introduced into the centre of the pitstead, which was then left to burn. As the wood charred the dome collapsed and required constant attention. Shifts in the wind made it necessary to re-position bracken hurdles, making it a very arduous occupation.

The advent of cylindrical kilns, with controllable air vents, proved a welcome alternative and they were more efficient. A great slump in production followed the conversion of the iron industry to coke, but in recent years the increasing popularity of the barbecue has re-kindled the trade. A new generation of charcoal burners has taken to the woods.

Stott Park Bobbin Mill
NEAR WINDERMERE

This handsome engine at Stott Park Bobbin Mill never achieved the status that its appearance demands.

When the mill was built in 1835, a water wheel produced power for an overhead shaft and associated belts and powered up to 30 lathes. By 1858, when the Coward family leased the mill, a water turbine was in use. Water turbines continued to be used until 1941, when electric motors were installed. The engine, it is thought, was used to augment the power supply. It was built in the 1880s by William Bradley & Sons of Brighouse, near Halifax, and was probably bought secondhand.

The mill was initially a very successful venture and supplied the Lancashire textile industry with bobbins of many shapes and sizes. There were improvements in lathes and expansions of buildings, and by the time the engine was installed the mill was also making handles for tools and pickaxes as well as toggles.

It had been a logical decision to make use of the plentiful sawdust, wood shavings and offcuts to fuel the engine which could produce up to twenty horsepower. However, the boom years did not last and this handsome machine had only been employed when trade was good. When the mill closed in 1971, it had been covered with sawdust for many years.

MORRIS MEN
LOWICK GREEN

During the 1960s, interest in our cultural heritage grew and dancing traditions, which had been ignored for so long, enjoyed a revival. In response to this movement the Furness Morris Men were formed in 1963. They are still performing Mummers plays and Morris dances throughout the southern Lake District.

The dances are said to have originated as an exhortation to nature to bring fertility to the land, ensuring good harvests. The movement may have spread throughout Europe from the Middle East and India. The title Morris is thought to be a corruption of the word Moorish, used in this instance to mean foreign or outlandish. The number of people in the dance depends on the locality it derives from. Cotswold Morris requires six dancers, and Westmorland eight. Traditionally, the costume requires white trousers and shirt, green cummerbund, red baldric and waistcoat – an outfit very similar to those found in the Basque region of Spain. Furness Morris Men decorate the back of their waistcoats with motifs connected in some way to the Lake District.

Here they are performing a Bampton dance from the Cotswolds at Lowick Green. This scene would have been familiar to Shakespeare, who makes references to such dancing in several of his plays.

Woodturner
NEAR CONISTON

Working with wood is considered by many to be a most satisfying occupation because of the feel of the material, the aroma of the wood and the beauty of the end result. Mass production of such things as broom handles, chair legs and banister rails holds less appeal, but wood turning was a way of producing items in volume. Prior to the use of mechanical power, the pole lathe was used. This had a treadle mechanism, which activated a cord wrapped around the wood being turned. This left the operator's hands free to use his cutting tools.

The development of water power, using Lakeland's many rushing rivers and streams, gave rise to the use of belts running from overhead shafts down to the lathes in large workshops. Specially designed cutting knives made lathes more adaptable and suitable for making bobbins, pill boxes, mangle rollers and axe and screwdriver handles.

Skilled craftsmen have returned to traditional methods of making quality furniture, and items such as bowls, boxes, lamp bases, light pulls and doorknobs for the tourist and domestic market. The value of unique design, quality workmanship and materials is gaining appreciation in the modern world.

THE MAGIC OF
THE LAKE DISTRICT

Cumbria's Lake District is an area of magical beauty suffused with myths and legends. Wherever one stands in Lakeland, there is always an eye-catching sight to behold, breathtaking landscapes and ancient cottages, all saturated with history.

Autumn on the Fells
TROUTBECK

Late in August the evenings darken and begin to cool. The bracken hangs its head and golden patches streak the hillsides. Birch trees cling to their leaves in the strengthening winds and the rowan prepares to offer up its berries.

By September the sun picks out fast deepening hues of gold, orange and rust brown, displayed beautifully against the dour grey crags. Lower down the valley sides squirrels collect nuts and badgers forage for berries, while up on the high ridges the red deer become restless. Puff balls and other fungi appear everywhere – their musty odour wafting on the breeze.

The sun appears lower on the horizon, deepening the colours as the bracken, now rusted, falls back towards the earth. The bright red berries of the rowan have been consumed by hungry birds and their seeds cast widely over the fellside. Mosses and lichens offer a contrast to the golden scene, and the deer begin to roar.

Rain falls steadily clouding the hilltops and swelling the streams and tarns. The bare trees darken. Soon it will be winter.

River Leven
WINDERMERE

The River Leven starts at the bottom end of Lake Windermere and flows in a south-westerly direction. It is a spectacular sight, with its densely wooded banks and swirling water. The Leven is very popular with tourists, and has been so for many decades.

In the nineteenth century, Lakeland became a highly popular spot for businessmen who had made their fortune as a result of the Industrial Revolution. The new class of moneyed industrialists, created a novel tier in Britain's social structure, a hitherto unheard of respectability and high social standing for those whose parentage was unremarkable, but whose business acumen was acute. Many of these newly rich families chose to buy second homes away from the smoke-belching, dirty cities from whence their wealth derived and the Lake District became one of the most popular spots. The southern shores of Lake Windermere and the banks of the River Leven witnessed the building of many nineteenth-century villas; many of these holiday homes can still be seen today, nestling in the woodland.

Hallin Fell and Ullswater
ULLSWATER

Hallin Fell is hugely popular with walkers and climbers. It is one of the easiest climbs in the Lake District, yet still provides the walker with a feeling of well-earned satisfaction. There are other, more difficult ways in which to reach the fell's summit, but the easy route also happens to be one of the most beautiful, leading as it does from the grassy slopes of Martindale Hause on the eastern side of Ullswater.

While ascending to the summit, walkers should pause to view the bewitching sight of Lake Ullswater and the scenic view over Howtown Bay. On particularly clear days it is also possible to look across the lake to Eden Valley, reputedly the most fertile land in Cumbria and the area that inspired the metaphysical poet Michael Drayton (1563–1631) who wrote:

O my bright lovely Brook, whose name doth
bear the sound of God's first garden-plot.

St Bees Head
ST BEES

St Bees Head is a rocky promontory above the coastal village of St Bees. When standing at the Head, one can see the village below. On turning to the opposite direction, one looks out over the Irish Sea.

In 1973 the 'Coast to Coast' walk was devized by Alfred Wainwright. His walk has since become famous. Each year thousands of walkers trek the 190 mile distance between the starting point at St Bees (remembering to wet their walking boots in the Irish Sea for good luck before setting out) and the finishing point of Robin Hood's Bay, on the North Sea.

The cliffs that form St Bees Head have been sculpted over many millennia by the waves of the Irish Sea and the force of the strong local winds. They are home to many species of plant and animal life and are the only place in Britain where the Black Guillemot breeds. As a result, the head has been turned into a nature reserve to give greater protection to its inhabitants.

Leven Estuary
WINDERMERE

This stunning view of the sands of Leven Estuary, seen from behind distinctive rust-coloured rocks, was photographed from Roudsea Wood, a National Nature Reserve and one of Cumbria's finest woodlands. The estuary is created by the River Leven, which flows into the sea at Morecambe Bay, in an area known as Greenodd Sands. At one time Greenodd was a port and shipbuilding yard but, due to silting, no boats larger than a yacht can now enter the bay.

Many years ago there was a gunpowder mill at Low Wood, not far from the Leven Estuary – the gunpowder was produced mainly for mining explosives and not for warfare. There was a more sinister side to the industry, however, a side of which the gunpowder workers were totally unaware. A vital raw ingredient of gunpowder is saltpetre, which was brought from the United States in vast quantities. The ships that brought it would then sail to Africa on their homeward routes – supplying gunpowder to the African mines and collecting slaves to take home to America. Thus the small Lakeland district of Greenodd unwittingly played part in the atrocious trade in human beings.

Rydal Water and Nab Scar
RYDAL

January 31st, Sunday

We walked round the two lakes. Grasmere was very soft, and the Rydale was extremely beautiful from the western side. Nab Scar was just topped by a cloud which, cutting it off as high as it could be cut off, made the mountain look uncommonly lofty.

from the journals of Dorothy Wordsworth

Rydal Water is a relatively small lake, connected to the larger Grasmere Lake by a slim footpath. Upon Rydal Water reside several small islands and an abundance of birds. This area was extremely popular with both Wordsworths and their oft-visiting friend, Samuel Taylor Coleridge.

The word 'scar' (or 'scarth') is an old English word for a sheer rock face. Nab Scar is a craggy rock face overlooking Rydal Water. On one of its slopes stands Nab Cottage, one-time home of the writer Thomas De Quincey, best known for his controversial novel *Confessions of an English Opium Eater*.

Rydal Water can be seen to great advantage from Rydal Mount, the one-time home of Wordsworth, and the site of the study in which he wrote while he was Poet Laureate.

Skiddaw and Derwentwater
DERWENTWATER

John Constable (1776—1837), the most famous English landscape artist of all time, spent several months in the Lake District and painted many scenes around this area. Perhaps the best known is his magnificent *Storm over Derwentwater*. Constable is the recognized master of landscape painting in the style known as Romantic. He painted directly from nature, performing his art in the open air instead of the oppressive and unnatural atmosphere of a studio – this was very unusual in the eighteenth and early nineteenth centuries.

Constable was born in Suffolk and showed an aptitude for painting from a very young age. As a school-age child, he helped his father in the family flour mill before leaving Suffolk for London, and the Royal Academy School, at the age of thirteen. At that time, the Royal Academy was the only school in England where artists were taken seriously.

The first exhibition of Constable's landscape paintings took place in 1802, although the reaction in his native England was not encouraging. In fact, Constable was barely appreciated in England at all during his lifetime. In France, however, his work became highly sought after and his open-air style was a major influence on two important groups of artists, the Barbizons and the Impressionists.

Town End
TROUTBECK

During the sixteenth century the price of wool rose 500 per cent. Farmers who had large flocks prospered and built new houses to reflect their status and wealth.

Town End is one such house. Now owned by the National Trust it was built between 1623 and 1626 by George Browne and was inhabited by the Browne family until the 1940s. It is a substantial Statesman's house, with all the trappings of gentry, befitting the family's position in local society. Externally, the house retains its rounded chimneys, drip stones and corbelled chimney stack, but there are alterations, including larger 'improved' mullioned windows.

The interior is, however, most impressive. The furnishings are large and imposing with carved tester beds and a huge table built in situ. Panelling and family paintings adorn the walls. The family assumed its own coat of arms, which is seen carved on many pieces. One George Browne was an enthusiastic wood carver who decorated furniture. He also added new pieces and joined them together to make them appear built-in.

Time appears to have stood still in this house. Each generation has treasured and retained the best of past times and it remains largely as the family left it.

Stock Ghyll Waterfall
AMBLESIDE

This cascading waterfall is about half a mile from the centre of the pretty village of Ambleside. The waterfall tumbles down 22 metres of jagged rock face and moss-covered boulders; it is a spectacular sight and surprising to stumble upon so close to a town centre.

Not far from Stock Ghyll Waterfall is Loughrigg Fell, a majestic mountain that rises to almost 340 metres. Near the mountain's foot stands Fox How house, the one-time home of Dr Thomas Arnold, a great friend of William Wordsworth, and father of the poet Matthew Arnold. Thomas Arnold (1795—1842) was Rugby School's most famous and influential headmaster. At a time when public schools stuck to a rigidly formal classical curriculum, he was forward-looking enough to introduce modern languages, mathematics, history, poetry and philosophy to the boys' education. His reforms brought about a radical change throughout the entire English education system.

Having been brought up in such a progressive household, it is no surprise that Matthew Arnold became a prolific scholar, poet and critic. He was educated at Rugby (where he later returned to teach Classics) and went to the University of Oxford. His works include many highly respected essays, but perhaps the best-known and most inspirational of all his works is the wonderful poem 'Dover Beach'.

Lake Buttermere and Fleetwith Pike
BUTTERMERE

Perfectly reflected here in the still waters of Lake Buttermere is the imposing Fleetwith Pike. The starkness of winter's snow accentuates the rugged peaks and sloping contours of the mountain – a splendid contrast to the unruffled surface of Buttermere. This view of the peaceful valley in western Lakeland may be seen from a walk that encircles the lake, all on accommodating paths close to the shore.

Fleetwith Pike rises to a height of 648 metres and is hugely popular with the thousands of climbing enthusiasts who swarm to the Lake District each year. The mountain is laced with a fascinating honeycomb of tunnels which were formed by the slate works of centuries past. For many hundreds of years labourers mined the unforgiving stone from the sides of the mountain. The stone was sold on to various industries, eventually to be used for roofs and floors, to be laid as paving slabs and to make blackboards for schools and writing slates for pupils.

Alongside the mountain is a valley through which stretches Honister Pass, a steep road that links the valleys of Buttermere and Borrowdale.

Reflections
DERWENTWATER

Derwentwater is one of the Lake District's most awe-inspiring bodies of water and has been sketched and photographed by millions. The lake is roughly three miles long and one mile wide and, at its deepest point, measures 22 metres. Within this frame lie four islands: Derwent Isle, Lord's Island, Rampsholme Island and St Herbert's Island. These have a fascinating history and have been host to many a Lakeland adventure. St Herbert's was once the home of a Celtic hermit who was later beatified and his name chosen for the island he once inhabited. Derwent Island was once inhabited by a colony of German miners who worked in the nearby copper mines.

Every summer, on Regatta Day, a staged sea battle, complete with cannons, took place on one of the islands. Two armies would be chosen, one of which would be the

island's inhabitants and the other, the attackers. This elaborate charade was a throwback to the time of the Norse invasions of around the tenth century. The mock battle was fought 'to the death', cheered on by high-spirited locals eager to witness the 'defeat' of the invading hordes.

River Duddon
FROM BIRKS BRIDGE

The River Duddon is a noted fishing river, rich in salmon and sea trout – a mesmerising place to rest and contemplate nature. William Wordsworth wrote many Duddon Sonnets and the following lines were composed while he sat on the River's bank:

Child of the clouds! Remote from every taint
Of sordid industry thy lot is cast;
Thine are the honours of the lofty waste.
William Wordsworth

Birks Bridge is a narrow crossing point that rises dramatically above Duddon Waterfalls. Not far away are the preserved remains of an old forge. The iron, which was worked at the forge, was transported along the River Duddon. The wood needed to stoke the blacksmith's fire came from the densely wooded banks of the river.

As can be seen from this photograph, the banks of the River Duddon are rocky, which can be dangerous in bad weather; nevertheless, the area is one of outstanding beauty to which many thousands of local people and holidaymakers are attracted each year. The good fishing in the river has been a lure to habitation for many centuries. Archaeologists have found human remains dating back many millennia in the area surrounding Birks Bridge.

Lodore Falls
BORROWDALE

Collecting, projecting
Receding and speeding
And shocking and rocking,
And darting and parting
Robert Southey, 'The Cataract of Lodore'

Made famous by Robert Southey's effusive verse, Lodore Falls have become a hugely popular tourist attraction. Large numbers of literary pilgrims and nature lovers take trips to this spell-binding area of Borrowdale each year.

Lodore Falls were created by the waters of an erratic stream which flows from Watendlath Tarn into Derwentwater. In this picture, taken after a period of rainfall has swelled the current, the waters are seen in all their splendour. Along its course, the flow of the water fluctuates dramatically, depending on local weather patterns: after heavy rain the Falls make a spectacular sight – cascading over rocks with small branches dragged along by the current; however, in a time of drought, they may disappear altogether. The following verse, the origins of which are unknown, records this phenomenon:

A dry season tourist once sought to explore,
Where doth the water come down to Lodore.
Quoth a Cumbrian maid with a toss of her bonnet,
You may well seek Lodore, for you're sitting upon it.

Brotherswater
FROM KIRKSTONE PASS NEAR PATTERDALE

It is said that a time long forgotten, two young brothers who should have been working at their tasks on the farm, were tempted on to the frozen lake. The result was a tragic accident, for both perished and Broadwater, or Broader Water, gained a new name in their memory.

The truth or otherwise of this legend will never be known, but there is no gloomy atmosphere at this gem of a lake. Wordsworth was so enamoured of this spot that he wrote a poem about it while contemplating the scene from Cow Bridge.

Viewed from Kirkstone Pass, the lake nestles at the base of a great rock-strewn glaciated valley. Mixed woodland fringes the lake's western shore where the hillside plunges steeply into the clear waters. Across the lake the hamlet of Hartsop is hidden among the trees. Running from their rushy fringes the hay fields direct one's sight to the mountains of High Street and the old Roman road. Walking from Ambleside over Scandale the terrain is more gentle than the route via Kirkstone, with rowan trees and cascading water upon which one's eyes can roam.

Not far from Brotherswater is Ullswater, a place where peace and beauty lies waiting for those who care to tread its paths and the thought of which draws travellers on.

Autumn Woodland
GRASMERE

The area around Grasmere is extraordinarily beautiful: the Vale of Grasmere is circled by mountains, valleys and airy woodland in which many a long, rewarding walk may be taken and scores of contented hours spent in daydreaming. As the woods around Grasmere were local to the Wordsworth children, they spent much of their life under the shelter of these trees. Nearby was a rock, 'the Rock of Names' or 'Sara's Rock' as it is referred to in Dorothy Wordsworth's writings. On this rock, the names 'Dorothy', 'William', 'Coleridge', 'Mary' and 'Sara' are all carved: Mary was William Wordsworth's wife and Sara was her sister. The rock was a popular meeting place for their group and is mentioned many times in Dorothy's diaries.

The distinguished English novelist E. M. Forster visited the Lake District in 1907, when he stayed in Grasmere for a few months. He took many walks around the surrounding woods and hills and commented that, in spite of incessant rain ('all night and every day, but not always all day'), he had grown very attached to the area.

Red Screes
KIRKSTONE PASS NEAR PATTERDALE

A curtain of rain glides over the whaleback mountain of Red Screes and sinks downwards to the valley below. It has already burdened Windermere and Ambleside with a downpour and, propelled by the south west winds, makes relentless progress.

In the wake of the rain patches of sun struggle weakly to the earth in an attempt to melt the last of the winter snows. Wet walkers climb to the summit whilst sheep stand stoically above the sodden ground. This is a watershed where rivers rise and flow their separate ways. The expansive hilltops soak up the rain greedily. The mountain is renowned for standing water and rushing streams.

Below, on the pass, views of the mountain are obscured by rain; even the famous Kirkstone loses its attraction when so saturated with water. Only the lakes Ullswater and Brotherswater rejoice at the rain, whilst tourists watch, hoping for clearer skies.

Cataract
ANGLE TARN BECK PATTERDALE

The Patterdale Valley is named after St Patrick, who lived sometime between the end of the fourth century and the sixth century. According to local legends, the patron saint of Ireland was shipwrecked in the turbulent waters and washed up on Duddon Sands. Local history dates this incident as AD540, despite the fact that it is generally accepted that he lived between AD385–461. Nevertheless, there is a church in the valley dedicated to St Patrick, on the site where he purportedly preached to the people who lived in the area and baptized those who converted to Christianity.

This breathtaking image shows a typical Lakeland scene – the feathery waterfall caused by a stream being diverted by rocks and dividing into rivulets. Cataracts such as this one are a common sight within the region, they are seen at their best after prolonged periods of heavy rain, when the waters gush over jagged stones.

Taylor Gill Force
BORROWDALE

This spectacular view of Taylor Gill Force shows one of the Lake District's most magnificent waterfalls (or 'forces' as they are called locally). The word 'Gill' means 'ravine', and derives from the language of Borrowdale's ancient Norse settlers. From the picturesque waterfall, walkers can take a slender path which leads up to Great Gable mountain.

Great Gable reaches a height of almost 900 metres and is the perfect place to stand in contemplation of the serene views below. Each year, on Remembrance Sunday, a large number of people gather at the mountain's summit in a poignant act of commemoration to honour the lives of those who have fallen in war. Marking the spot of the Remembrance Day service is a memorial to local people who died in the two World Wars.

According to legend, in times gone past the people of Borrowdale so dreaded the onset of winter and its harsh weather, that they came up with a scheme to ensure they would enjoy constant summer. Their plan involved the building of a massive wall that ran all along the bottom end of the Borrowdale Valley – the wall was intended to keep out the despised herald of winter, the cuckoo.

Nab Cottage
RYDAL

Nab Cottage was built in 1556. It is sited on a lower slope of the mountain Nab Scar. The cottage has been inhabited for many centuries but is most famous for its early nineteenth-century tenant, the English writer Thomas De Quincey. De Quincey achieved fame, and notoriety, with his controversial novel *Confessions of an English Opium Eater.*

De Quincey married Margaret Simpson, the daughter of Nab Cottage's previous owner – a match of which William Wordsworth wholly disapproved on the grounds of Margaret being a farmer's daughter! Despite the Poet Laureate's disapprobation (he even went so far as to write to De Quincey's mother for support), De Quincey and his wife were together for many happy years, some of which were spent in this house. Perhaps as a reproach to Wordsworth for his attempt to stop the marriage De Quincey wrote another controversial book, *Recollections of the Lakes and the Lake Poets.*

Hartley Coleridge (1796–1849), eldest son of Samuel Taylor Coleridge and a great friend of both Dorothy and William Wordsworth, also lived here between 1841 and his death in 1849. He died in Nab Cottage at the age of just 43. Like his father, he was a poet and eminent scholar and achieved literary acclaim in his lifetime. His best-known work is a collection simply entitled *Poems.*

View to Scafell Pike
NEAR LANGDALE

The three tarns, which lie at the pass between Bowfell and Crinkle Crags, mark the parting of the ways to Eskdale and Great Langdale.

Looking west towards the upper Esk valley the highest mountains in England dominate the skyline. The mountains are places of barren stone and scree – a sharp contrast to the boggy waters of the tarn. The huge bulk of Scafell lies to the left and is easily ascended by some paths, but there are some precipitous slopes and crags. The mountain top is bare and without shelter, but has magnificent views of other high mountains all around.

Far to the south and west the sea sparkles from Morecambe Bay to Ravenglass. The Isle of Man can sometimes be discerned through the clouds. The Solway Firth and Scotland appear in the north west and eastwards are the Coniston Fells. The bulk of Scafell Pike interrupts the panorama, standing 49 metres above its companions Broad Crag and Ill Crag. The highest peak in England, it entices walkers who first have to descend Scafell and cross the saddle of Mickledore to gain its summit. Much danger lies in store for the careless climber. Unsurpassed in their grandeur, however, these mountains stand supreme.

Pavey Ark
GREAT LANGDALE

The bleat of a lamb magnified and echoing from the face of Pavey Ark so startled Wordsworth that he was inspired to write about it.

This is a place of drama: the considerable volcanic outpourings that made these mountains were ravaged by huge glaciers, producing a spectacular combination of a wide, flat valley floor bordered by steep crags. Pavey Ark is a dark, brooding, rock wall, fissured by gullies and sheltering at its foot a small tarn. Slashed across the rock wall is a deep groove known as Jack's Rake, which offers the opportunity to scramble up the face – but this is not a place for the inexperienced or faint hearted. Water courses down the slope making the rocks slippery. The vegetation that survives the onslaught worms its roots far into the cracks. Once the summit is achieved an expansive view reveals Windermere Lake in all its splendour. Far below is the valley floor bordered by steeply rising fells.

Harris on Stickle and Pike O'Stickle complement Pavey Ark and together they form probably the most recognizable group of mountains in the Lake District: that of the Langdale Pikes.

Little Langdale Tarn
LITTLE LANGDALE

Little Langdale is restful to the eye and soothing to the soul. It is a nicely balanced valley with lovely views and complementary buildings of a pleasing scale.

The tarn is a place to relax and enjoy the scene on a warm sunny day. Viewed from this point, Pike O'Blisco is the dominating fell. The slopes of Lingmoor Fell are to the right, and Great Carrs to the left. There is a contrast in hues between the long-held colours of the bracken of the fellside and the green pastures fringing the lake. Streams race down the hillsides where the infant River Brathay enters from Wrynose. It runs calmly and passes under Slaters Bridge, named after the men who walked over it to work in the nearby quarries.

At Tilberthwaite the beck allows itself to be forded. Soon the valley steepens and within a mile of the tarn is Colwith Force, a small waterfall down which the river cascades on its journey to Lake Windermere.

Humphrey Head
NEAR GRANGE-OVER-SANDS

Humphrey Head is just a little way along the coast from the village of Grange-over-Sands. It is an impressive cliff looking out over the waters of Morecambe Bay and is one of the highest points on the West coast of England. According to local legend, the last wolf in Cumbria was slain here. From Humphrey Head Point, a peak jutting out over the sea, one has unsurpassed views across the water – on a clear day the Isle of Man may be spotted from the cliff top.

When the tide goes out at Morecambe Bay, it *really* goes out, leaving a huge area of sand exposed. For centuries locals have taken advantage of the great fishing opportunities this allows. Scores of fishers walk the sands at low tide to catch shrimps and flook (pronounced 'fluke'), a type of flatfish, that become stranded in shallow pools. At one time, people would arrive at the sands with their horses and carts, but today the fishers use tractors. However the sands of Morecambe Bay can be treacherous, with large pockets of quicksand – on occasion the sand has been known to swallow whole tractors.

View of the Valley
DUDDON

The Duddon Valley offers a variety of scenes along its entire length, all very pleasing. It is therefore not surprising that Wordsworth described the Duddon as his favourite river. The infant river rises upon Wrynose Fell, changing its mood and speed as it winds, then falls, to enter the gorge that skirts Wallowbarrow Crag. Picking a tortuous path around the tumbled boulders that form deep pools and shingle banks, the river calms and enters the scene before us.

This was a scene familiar to 'Wonderful Walker', who spent all his life in the valley. As vicar of Seathwaite and the local schoolmaster he was famed for his goodness of heart and temper, his industry and kindness. His spinning wheel was in constant use and his shearing stone is by the church.

In summer the crag is cloaked thickly in fresh green foliage. Down in the valley near its foot ants busy themselves heaving bits of wood. Unexpected stepping stones invite exploration of the valley. By the river are lazy pools suitable for swimming and fishing, similar to those found on the fellsides above.

Victorian Postbox
WASDALE HEAD

Set into a drystone wall at Wasdale Head is one of the country's earliest postboxes, dating from the time of Queen Victoria who reigned from 1837–1901. Set above the opening are the letters *V R*, on either side of a royal crown: this is an abbreviation of *Victoria Regina*, latin for Queen Victoria.

Before the arrival of postboxes, letters had to be taken to the post office from where they were guaranteed to be delivered by hand. Sending letters was thus expensive. However, with the successful re-introduction of the Penny Post on 6 May 1840, a cheap, efficient postal service was available to all. In 1852, to keep up with the demand, Britain's Royal Mail service announced its newest invention: 'pillar boxes' for posting letters. On 23 November of the same year, the first of these remarkable new designs was unveiled, in the Channel Island town of St Helier on Jersey. Soon there were pillar boxes throughout the British Isles and 'pillar box red' became a fashionable colour for garments. Today the distinctive red colour and classic design is a common and much-loved sight around Britain.

Friars' Crag and Causey Pike
DERWENTWATER

The sight of Derwentwater from Friars' Crag is probably the best known of all Lake District views. The crag takes its name from the many monks who used to come to this point on their pilgrimage to St Herbert's Island on Derwentwater. This photograph, in which a perfect reflection of Causey Pike, hemmed by a lush border of deep green pine trees can be seen, was taken in the crisp light of a perfect September morning.

Friar's Crag was bought as a memorial, commemorating the life and works of Canon Rawnsley, one of Keswick's nineteenth-century parsons – a lifelong friend of Beatrix Potter and a founder of the National Trust. The Canon was also the Trust's first Secretary, a position he filled for a great many years.

On Friars' Crag itself there is a stone memorial to another famous Lakeland dweller, John Ruskin. The memorial bears the following inscription, taken from Ruskin's book *Modern Painters*:

The first thing which I remember as an event in my life was being taken by my nurse to the brow of Friars' Crag on Derwentwater.

John Ruskin

132

Derwentwater
FROM SURPRISE VIEW

Surprise View is an outstanding viewpoint located on the road that runs from Watendlath to Borrowdale. One can look down many hundreds of feet to a glistening mirror that is Derwentwater. Surprise View also rewards walkers with spectacular views of Skiddaw.

Derwentwater lies amid grand fells and mysterious woodland and has captured the imagination of writers, artists and, more recently, photographers for many centuries. Along the shores of Derwentwater lies the town of Keswick, an area which has been popular as a settlement for many hundreds of years. Its name derives from a combination of two languages – Norse and Old English – hinting at a diverse history of inhabitants. The word 'Keswick' actually means 'cheese farm', and attests to an early agricultural community. It was in the eighteenth century that Keswick finally made the leap from small market town to the centre of tourism one can visit today.

Birchwood
BORROWDALE

Borrowdale Birches is a notable old natural woodland beside the River Derwent. It is a site of great peace, with dappled sunlight breaking through ancient branches, and a place where silver birch trees flourish. Walkers prefer to take the picturesque footpath through the woods, thereby avoiding the narrow valley road. Many attractive places to sit and picnic can be found along the river's lush banks.

The woods and fells around Borrowdale can often be seen mirrored on the surface of Cumbria's magnificent Derwentwater. The lake is famed for the quality of its reflections and for its mysterious 'floating island'. Derwentwater is home to four islands. However, about once every three years, a fifth island appears at the lake's south-west corner. This ghostly phenomenon was long the cause of much local superstition, but can be explained without recourse to romantic notions: the island is a mingled collection of water vegetation and weeds, and the force that keeps it bouyant is a build up of gases from the nearby marsh land.

Borrowdale Fells and Scafell Range
BORROWDALE

Borrowdale Fells can be seen here from a well-known footpath that links Walla Crag and Ashness Bridge. In the distance are the Lake District's highest mountains known collectively as the Scafell Range. These striking fells rise up to an average of 900 metres and provide climbers and walkers with spectacular views. The highest peak in the range, Scafell Pike, is also the highest mountain in England.

During the Victorian era, hill walking grew considerably in popularity attracting town dwellers out to the countryside. Where formerly only country people would have walked a route, tourists began arriving to do the same. Much of this change had to do with the Industrial Revolution when journeys between town and country became more easy and cross-over societies emerged. As machines took over agricultural work thousands upon thousands of agricultural labourers were forced to move into urban areas to find work. This influx into towns resulted in urban dwellers hearing about the countryside, its beauties and wonderful pastimes, and lured many to settle there.

Skiddaw and Keswick
FROM WALLA CRAG

This view of Keswick, the Lake District's northern capital, can be seen from the summit of Walla Crag. The journey is a popular and not-too-strenuous walk from the outskirts of the town. The mountain, providing this scene with its dramatic backdrop, is Skiddaw, the summit of which, at 930 metres, towers impressively above Keswick and its surrounding area. Skiddaw's smooth slopes are in stark contrast to the harsh slate rocks found on Walla Crag.

Keswick is renowned for its popularity with the Lakeland Poets, one of whom was Robert Southey (1774–1843). He resided for a while with Samuel Taylor

Coleridge at Greta Hall, Keswick, where with their friend Richard Lovell, they discussed their utopian ideals. The trio planned to found an idyllic community in the USA in Pennsylvania. Sadly nothing ever came of their grand scheme.

Coleridge and Southey married two sisters, although Coleridge's union was a deeply unhappy one. Abandoning his dreams of North America, Southey, with his wife, left for Portugal where his time was occupied writing poetry. Later he returned to England and, in 1813, was appointed Poet Laureate. Coleridge also travelled the world, but the lure of the Lakes was too strong and he returned to his family and the Keswick area.

Eskdale Valley
FROM HARTER FELL DUDDON VALLEY

The upper reaches of the Eskdale Valley are some of the most remote areas of the Lake District. Eskdale has no vehicular access for approximately half its length and visitors who travel over Hardknott Pass are often unaware that the river they have left behind cuts deeply into the mountains to the north. The track to Upper Eskdale passes through land once managed by the monks of Furness Abbey. The farm has existed here for centuries and its name has Norse connotations.

Beyond Brotherilkeld there is a large area of grazing through which the River Esk flows, either side are steep crags. In summer, the pasture is awash with wild flowers. At Throstle Garth an old pack horse bridge spans the river and affords excellent opportunities to view nearby cascades.

Ahead is Great Moss, where the river wanders across large stony areas, after which the valley rises steeply and the route divides.

One route leads to Mickledore and Scafell, but the true head of the valley is the pass named Esk Hause. From here routes lead to Wasdale, Borrowdale, Langdale and Scafell Pike. Spectacular views are afforded by any of these tracks; to travel up this valley is to experience one of Lakeland's true delights.

Coppice Woodland
NEAR LYNDALE

Ransom is perhaps a kinder name than wild garlic, as this plant is more commonly known. Wild garlic doesn't immediately bring to mind the distinctive odour of this beautiful plant. Snow white flowers rise above dark green leaves and tumble through the wood spreading further each year. As the sun streams in through the branches above, the whiteness intensifies and the deer and badger paths become more noticeable.

At this time of year there are still some bluebells and the tree foliage is fresh and bright. Looking at such a tranquil scene it is hard to imagine how busy this place once was. Down the track which passes through is an old lime kiln and there are large areas of coppiced hazel and ash.

This scene is typical of southern Lakeland: the industry has disappeared and nature is reclaiming the land. Wildlife is plentiful, birds are to be seen in great variety and the wood offers new beauties in each season.

Cowmire Hall
WINSTER VALLEY

Cowmire Hall is a Grade II listed building and one of the most attractive private houses anywhere in the Lake District. The first building work on this site took place in the sixteenth century, when a defensive pele tower was erected where the hall now stands. The walls of the tower now form the rear section of the present-day mansion. The hall's frontage was added on in the seventeenth century, creating a dramatically combined structure unlike that of any other building in Lakeland.

As well as the quaint, rose-adorned door seen in this photograph, the front of Cowmire Hall boasts seventeen mullioned windows. If one ventures inside, the interior of the large farmhouse is no less attractive than its outward appearance: there are some wonderful seventeenth-century features, including superb fireplaces. Above one of these remains an ancient coat of arms, that of the Le Fleming family, who were one time owners of Cowmire Hall and a prominent local family with French ancestry.

Today, Cowmire (pronounced 'Coomer' by the locals) is owned by the Barrett family, the ancestors of whom owned the Coniston Copper Mines several generations back.

Loughrigg Tarn
LANGDALE

Pictured here, reflecting of a fresh English sky, is Loughrigg Tarn, a haven of rare woodland species and water birds and much-loved by ornithologists. Tarns (once described as eyes of the mountains) are small lakes created in mountainous regions. The word 'tarn' comes from the Old English once widely spoken in this region.

Loughrigg Tarn is an attractive body of water that resides in a hollow on the side of Loughrigg Fell, not far from Skelwith Bridge. The water of this idyllic mountain lake is usually as still as it appears in this image and the views from its shores provide wonderful glimpses of Langdale Pikes. Now owned by the National Trust, the area around Loughrigg Tarn seems set to remain an oasis of peace and serenity.

Walked to Ambleside in the evening round the lake, the prospect exceedingly beautiful from Loughrigg Fell. It was so green that no eye could be weary of reposing upon it.

**from the journals of
Dorothy Wordsworth**

Causey Pike
FROM COLEDALE HORSESHOE NEAR KESWICK

There are many so-called 'horseshoe' passes throughout the Lake District – here one can see one of the most beautiful, Coledale Horseshoe as viewed from Causey Pike. The horseshoe-shaped pass was formed after the last Ice Age. When the glaciers that had formed (from mountains which were higher then than they are today) began to melt, the force of the water created deep ravines in the land. Due to the formation of the Lake District's hills and fells, the water's natural course took many sloping turns, creating the distinctive semi-circular passes so admired today. The district's great lakes were also formed in this way – formed, that is, by the sheer force of water whose way forward was blocked by silt or earlier glacial flow, thus corroding deep into the land.

The Coledale Valley was an area of great importance during the Middle Ages. Within this region several precious metals could be mined, providing a valuable source of local income.

Sour Milk Ghyll
EASEDALE GRASMERE

There are several streams in Lakeland with the name 'Sour Milk'. This one is at Easedale, not far from William Wordsworth's childhood stamping ground of Grasmere. The source of this Sour Milk Ghyll is Easedale Tarn, a tiny sheet of water left in a hanging valley, cupped in a hollow formed by glaciers during the last Ice Age.

A few miles from this spot stands Dunmail Raise, named after the last king of Cumberland. This site marks his defeat at the hands of Edmund, King of Northumbria in AD945. Edmund was from a victorious warring family – his ancestor was Edwin of Northumbria, one of the few early rulers to gain power over the Scots and whose name lives on in the name Edinburgh.

Dunmail Raise was the hill climbed by Wordsworth and De Quincey during the Peninsular War of the early 1900s. They walked to the top of Dunmail Raise to secure a paper delivered by coach from London. In anticipation of the news, Wordsworth lay down with his ear to the ground and was able to tell De Quincey when the coach was on its way.

Wastwater
WASDALE HEAD

Wonderful Wastwater presents a different face of the Lake District. It is famous for the steeply plunging screes that fall 340 metres into the deepest of the Lakes. At its head are the highest mountains.

When the sky is blue and the waters calm, mirror images reflect the majesty of the scene. When the weather is less clement the lake takes on a desolate forbidding face, which brought fear to the hearts of early visitors.

The valley sides are stony and treeless: the glacier has swept and smoothed their slopes. At the valley head a wide flat expanse of land houses the small community of Wasdale Head. Vast piles of rock bear witness to the clearance in earlier days of ice -borne stone from the 345 acres of communal pasture-land. A patchwork of walls encloses fields and points to 32 ancient yew trees that surround the tiny church.

Travellers used this valley route to reach the high passes beyond, and climbers and walkers ventured on to the slopes of the impressive high fells, including Great Gable and Scafell.

Coniston Fells and Coniston Water
CONISTON

Coniston Lake has a lovely shoreline – there are luxuriant mixed woodlands with birds, animals and plants in profusion, pebbly beaches from which to bathe and picnic, sweeping meadows and rocks and caves. It is a peaceful place, for there are no powered craft, apart from the steam yacht *Gondola*, which, Arthur Ransome claimed, the captain let him steer when a boy.

The valley sides do not press in as in other valleys and this allows for many and varied views. The most imposing is the view with Coniston Old Man at its centre, Dow Cragg to the left and Wetherlam to the right.

The people of the valley used the wood for their industries burning charcoal, smelting iron, stripping bark and making poles and besoms. The rural scene amidst such beauty drew writers and artists in large numbers. John Ruskin built his home at Brantwood, and Arthur Ransome lived nearby. Lewis Carroll, Charles Darwin, Matthew Arnold and Edward Lear were among the many visitors to Coniston Water. Tennyson spent his honeymoon by the lakeside and Holman Hunt, Burne Jones and Turner came here to paint.

Coniston village does not have the shopping facilities that attract so many tourists, as do the main centres, so it is still possible to enjoy this lake and the views all alone.

Croglin Beck Waterfall
NEAR PENRITH

During the eleventh century Benedictine nuns founded a nunnery at Staffield, near Penrith. It was situated close to a beautiful wooded valley through which Croglin Beck flows to meet the River Eden. Nothing remains of the nunnery except for the name, which is attached to the house now found on the site.

The present Nunnery House was built by the Aglionby family during the eighteenth century. Christopher Aglionby was very much a man of his time: enamoured of the Romantic Movement. His heightened perception of the beauties of nature and the spirituality of man's relationship with it led him to create 'Nunnery Walks'.

The creation of paths giving access to the sublime experience of a series of cascades and falls in a wild and wooded valley prompted William Wordsworth to describe them as 'unrivalled in beauty'.

In 1794 a guidebook by Hutchinson, *A History of Cumberland* volume I, encouraged visitors to visit the largest fall:

...the noise of a cascade strikes the ear a few moments only before it bursts upon the sight. The scene is noble and solemn, branches of trees are stretched and mingled from precipice to precipice. The water gushes in one entire spout through the parted rock – you pass on enchanted.
William Hutchinson

This enchantment is still tangible today.

THE MAGIC & MYSTERY OF THE LAKE DISTRICT

LITERATURE & ART

An astounding number of writers and artists have found inspiration in the Lake District: Turner, Constable, Ruskin, Coleridge, Wordsworth and De Quincey to name just a few.

Dora's Field
RYDAL

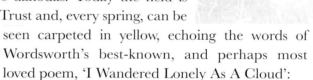

This plot of land lies near to William Wordsworth's home, Rydal Mount, the house he lived in from 1813 until his death in 1850. Wordsworth bought the field in 1826 and gave it to his daughter, Dora. When she died, sadly at a young age, the land became Wordsworth's property once again. He named it Dora's Field. The daffodils that grow in such profusion over the field are known as Wordsworth's daffodils. Today the field is owned by the National Trust and, every spring, can be seen carpeted in yellow, echoing the words of Wordsworth's best-known, and perhaps most loved poem, 'I Wandered Lonely As A Cloud':

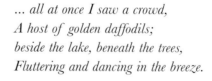

... all at once I saw a crowd,
A host of golden daffodils;
beside the lake, beneath the trees,
Fluttering and dancing in the breeze.

Continuous as the stars that shine
And twinkle on the Milky Way.
They stretched in never-ending line
Along the margin of the bay:
Ten thousand saw I at a glance,
Tossing their heads in sprightly dance ...

... oft, when on my couch I lie
In vacant or in pensive mood,
They flash upon the inward eye
Which is the bliss of solitude;
And then my heart with pleasure fills,
And dances with the daffodils
William Wordsworth,
'I Wandered Lonely as A Cloud'

Wordsworth's Grave
GRASMERE

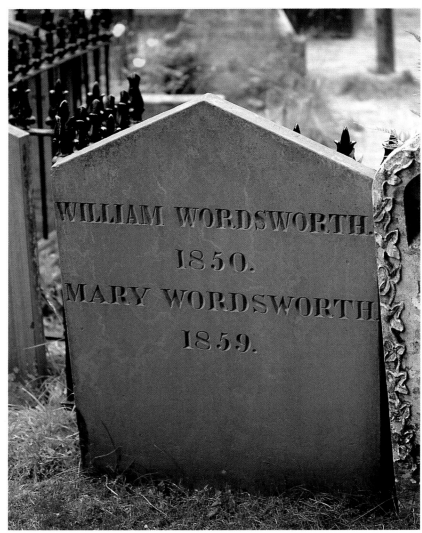

*... the earth
And common face of Nature spake to me
Rememberable things ...*
William Wordsworth

William Wordsworth was born in the Lakeland town of Cockermouth on 7 April 1770 and died in Rydal Mount, his final home (just a few miles away from the house of his birth) on 23 April 1850. He is buried in the graveyard of Grasmere's parish church along with his wife Mary, his sister Dorothy and other members of their family. Also buried in the yew-filled country churchyard is Hartley Coleridge, the son of the Wordsworths' great friend, Samuel Taylor Coleridge.

Wordsworth spent most of his life in the Lake District, although as a youth he lived for a while in France and, on one occasion, he and Dorothy accompanied Coleridge on a trip to Germany. Despite his enjoyment of France, Lakeland beckoned and the nature-loving poet always returned.

Surprisingly for one whose life was devoted to poetry, Wordsworth's gravestone reads very simply: it records his name, that of his wife and the years of their deaths. Today, thousands of literary pilgrims come to visit this grave each year, remembering England's best-known Romantic poet.

Wordsworth's Birthplace
COCKERMOUTH

William Wordsworth was born in this elegant Georgian house in the Cumbrian town of Cockermouth in 1770. Wordsworth House (as it is now named) was built in 1745, it has a beautifully laid-out terraced garden and stables. The garden of the house ran down to the River Derwent, a waterway by which William and his sister, Dorothy, often played. One of Wordsworth's most famous pieces of poetry is his epic, *The Prelude*, in which he writes of his childhood years in the Lake District. There are many specific references to the River Derwent, including the following lines:

That one, the fairest of all Rivers, lov'd
To blend his murmur's with my Nurse's song,
And from his alder shades and rocky falls,
And from his fords and shadows, sent a voice
That flow'd along my dreams.
William Wordsworth, 'The Prelude'

Today Wordsworth House is a museum devoted to Wordsworth memorabilia, and seven of the house's rooms can be seen furnished in true eighteenth-century style. There is a plaque at the house which reads:

In this house was born on April 7th 1770 William Wordsworth, Poet Laureate.
He died at Rydal Mount, Grasmere, April 23rd 1850, Interred in Grasmere
Churchyard. Dorothy, his sister, 1771-1855.

'Shootin' Moose' by Andy Frost
GRIZEDALE FOREST

The slightly surprised look on the face of the moose is mirrored in those seeing it for the first time. On subsequent visits, viewers' expressions change to eager anticipation – for this sculpture is fun.

Children are drawn to sit astride the gun barrel that aims into the woods, frightening away any nasty creatures lurking in the silent darkness of the trees. The moose provides a gentler aspect, as is its way, peering away from these terrors to survey the scene.

Constructed of local timber with addition of colour it could not, perhaps, be considered a response to the environment, as in some more esoteric sculptures. Together with Frost's depiction of a chieftain in a hot spot and the Indians which peer out from behind trees, it gives enormous pleasure and an added buzz to a walk in the forest.

'The Ancient Forester' by David Kemp

GRIZEDALE FOREST

Sculpture with a limited life was a fairly new idea in 1977 when the Grizedale Society Sculpture Project was founded with support from Northern Arts. Bill Grant MBE, who was chief forester, had the idea of encouraging young sculptors to live in a rural community for about six months. They are urged to respond to a natural forest environment, which offers so many sites, materials and habitats for them to explore and interpret in their own way. One of these sculptures, 'The Ancient Forester', is the dominant creature of the forest, an image of Man the Hunter. Described as 'a figure of great antiquity', he is a mystic, and guardian of the forest, his responsible husbandry in harmony with nature.

He stands to welcome people and other sculptures provide interest and enjoyment along the many trails. Constructed from oak this forester will probably outlive many of his companions, the creatures made of twisted roots and brushwood, softwood figures and structures. New sculptures are needed regularly, for time and weather take their toll. Of the 200 hopeful applicants who wish to take up this challenge each year, however, only four or five may realize their dream.

Helvellyn and Thirlmere
FROM ARMBOTH

Ye mountains and ye lakes
And sounding cataracts, ye mists and winds
That dwell among the hills where I was born.
If, mingling with the world, I am content
With my own modest pleasure and have lived
With God and Nature communing, removed
From little enmities and low desires
That gift is yours

William Wordsworth

The mountain of Helvellyn was often climbed by William and Dorothy Wordsworth and their friends. Dorothy mentions Helvellyn many times in her journals, which date back to the late eighteenth and early nineteenth centuries, and makes many references to walking with her brother and their friend Samuel Taylor Coleridge. On 25 October 1801 Dorothy wrote the following description of a trip up the mountain with her brother:

... sweet day. Went upon
Helvellyn, glorious glorious sights.
The sea at Cartmel. The Scotch
mountains beyond the sea to the
right. Whiteside large, and round,
and very soft , and green, behind
us. Mists above and below,
and close to us, with the Sun
amongst them.

from the journals of
Dorothy Wordsworth

154

Lake Windermere
FROM JENKYN'S CRAG

Lake Windermere is known as the longest lake in England, although, in reality, it is a 'mere' rather than a lake. It stretches for over 11 miles. There is no speed limit on the lake – the only watercourse in the Lake District not to have one imposed on it – and many water sports enthusiasts take advantage of the fact.

Windermere has long been a mecca for fans of water activities. All the Lake writers and artists appear to have spent many happy hours walking beside or boating on the lake. The following extract from Dorothy Wordsworth's journal of June 1802 describes how a typical day on Windermere might have been spent:

Ellen and I rode to Windermere. We had a
fine sunny day, neither hot nor cold....
I was enchanted with some of the views....
Then we went to the Island,
walked round it, and crossed the lake
with our horse in the ferry.

from the journals of
Dorothy Wordsworth

Jenkyn's Crag, from where this view of Windermere was taken, can be visited by an easy walk from Ambleside. The crag juts out across the head of Windermere, above Waterhead, and provides a dazzling panorama of the Lakeland hills.

Elterwater Tarn and Langdale Pikes
LANGDALE

The Elterwater area is one of the prime grazing pastures for the Lake District's prized Herdwick sheep. It is also the location of a now-defunct slate-quarrying industry and gunpowder factory. Elterwater Tarn can be found near Skelwith Bridge in the Langdale Valley. In this picture it is seen with the Langdale Pikes, three mountains (or fells) known individually as Harrison Stickle, Pike O'Stickle and Pavey Ark. Harrison Stickle is the highest; its summit reaches 736 metres and provides superb views over Elterwater and Langdale Valley. Collectively, the Langdale Pikes form the best-known silhouette in Lakeland.

Wordsworth and his friends often walked from Grasmere to Eltwater, where they spent their time fishing for perch. Dorothy records several trips to Elterwater in her journals, including the following entry from June 1800:

When Wm. went to the water to fish, I lay ... my head pillowed upon a mossy rock, and slept about 10 minutes, which relieved my headache. We ate our dinner together, and parted again. Wm. was afraid he had lost his line and sought me.... We sat on the side of the hill looking to Elterwater.

**from the journals of
Dorothy Wordsworth**

Coniston Water
NIBTHWAITE

Coniston Water was one of the favourite places of the novelist Arthur Ransome, who based much of his famous book *Swallows and Amazons* on the landscape and waters of the area. Around Nibthwaite was one of his favourite places. He spent much time here as a child and memories of the glorious surroundings came to the fore while he composed his adult works.

The celebrated artist J. M. W. Turner (1775–1851) was another fond visitor to the Coniston area. Turner travelled throughout the world and gained fame from his evocative landscapes, particularly those of Venice. The Lake District had a tremendous hold on his imagination and he spent many holidays walking the hills. His reputation was further enhanced by the patronage of another Lakeland dweller, John Ruskin, who praised his work enthusiastically in his *Modern Painters* of 1843. Today, London's Tate Gallery houses one of Turner's earliest works, his 'Morning amongst the Coniston Fells', produced in 1797, after a holiday in the Lake District.

Blea Tarn Cottage
LANGDALE

Blea Tarn Cottage is the home of a character in Wordsworth's epic poem *The Excursion*. The house is sited on a minor road between the valleys of Little Langdale and Great Langdale, on the side of Lingmoor Fell. The house's prime position means that it benefits from maximum sunlight in any day, including through the winter months.

> *...Within the circuit of this fabric huge,*
> *One voice – the solitary raven, flying*
> *Athwart the concave of the dark blue dome...*
> *... Faint – and still fainter – as the cry, with which*
> *The wanderer accompanies her flight*
> *Through the calm region, fades upon the ear*
> **William Wordsworth, The Excursion, book IV**

This area was also visited by Mrs Ann Radcliffe, a contemporary of Wordsworth's, though with a dramatically different writing style. Mrs Radcliffe lived between 1764 and 1823 and wrote four novels. Her books were at the forefront of the Gothic-Romance style. For a time she was England's most popular

novelist. Her writing includes *A Sicilian Romance*, *The Romance of the Forest*, *The Mysteries of Udolpho* and *The Italian*. Unlike Wordsworth, Mrs Radcliffe wrote that the Lakeland scenery filled her with 'horror' and was quick to return to her native London – no doubt formulating fresh Gothic plots as she journeyed away from the dramatic peaks, precipices and cataracts.

Ruskin's Study
BRANTWOOD

A single villa can mar a landscape and dethrone a dynasty of hills.
John Ruskin

John Ruskin lived at Brantwood for the last 28 years of his life: from 1872 until his death in 1900. The house has been preserved as it was in his time, still containing many of his own watercolours and sketches, as well as those by other, fine artists, whose work he collected.

In Ruskin's lifetime, he was a celebrated and much-revered public figure. He challenged and changed the consciousness of an entire nation and his house became the epicentre of nineteenth-century intellectualism. Many of society's most important figures visited Ruskin at Brantwood – men from all walks of life, including luminary greats such as Gandhi, Tolstoy and Proust, mingling and formulating ideas for a better world.

Ruskin was one of the most remarkable of men, not only of England and our time but of all countries and all times. ... He thought and said not only what he himself had seen and felt, but what everyone will think and say in the future.
Leo Tolstoy

Lake Bassenthwaite
BASSENTHWAITE NEAR KESWICK

Bassenthwaite is the only true lake in the entire Lake District – all the others are geographically either waters or meres. Bassenthwaite is a quiet lake, renowned for its salmon and trout fishing, with the lonely church of St Bega standing on the shore, at the foothills of Skiddaw, and the River Derwent meandering its way through, en route to the sea.

The area around Bassenthwaite Lake was one of those painted by the eminent English landscape artist John Constable, several of whose works now hang in Abbot's Hall Art Gallery in Kendal. Constable stayed in the Lake District in 1806, spending September to November as a guest of John Hardon at Braithway. During his stay, he was visited frequently by Southey and Coleridge, who were living at Keswick.

Constable toured the district widely and many of his most famous pictures were painted here. Constable took Thomas West's *Guide to the Lakes* (published in 1778 and the first Lakeland guide to be produced) with him and sketched almost everything West mentioned. He averaged two sketches a day using both watercolours and pencil. For the last three weeks of his tour Constable stayed at Borrowdale where he worked obsessively. Borrowdale and Rydale were also amongst the scenes he painted.

Troutbeck Park Farm
TROUTBECK

Troutbeck Park was the first farm in the Lake District to be owned by the celebrated children's author Beatrix Potter. The only daughter of wealthy, overbearing parents, Beatrix was allowed absolutely no freedom and led an unhappy, though materially privileged, childhood; her few happy memories of this time were all from holidays taken in the Lake District.

Potter wrote her first story for an ill child, a family friend. It was never intended for publication. It was another friend, Reverend Rawnsley (later Canon Rawnsley) who persuaded her to publish the work. From tenuous beginnings grew an empire of children's writing and worldwide renown. It also earned money – and therefore gave independence – to a sadly oppressed young woman. Troutbeck Farm became the symbol of this new-found independence and the home of Beatrix and her husband, Lakeland solicitor William Heelis.

Beatrix Potter's love and understanding of the country and animals can be seen in her writing. After a few years, she lessened her writing time, concentrating instead on breeding and rearing Herdwick sheep, indigenous to the Lake District. She became the first woman ever to be elected president of the Herdwick Sheep Breeders' Association.

When Beatrix died in 1943, Troutbeck Farm, and more than 4000 acres of land, were left to the National Trust, one of whose founding members was Canon Rawnsley.

Village Centre
GRASMERE

Grasmere is a picturesque village, with ancient houses and rich in tradition and local culture. There is the annual rushbearing ceremony (much loved by Wordsworth), regular Wordsworthian festivals and wrestling matches. Wordsworth once taught at the small village school, which has since become a shop and is constantly filled with the enticing smell of freshly baked gingerbread, a local delicacy.

The Wordsworth siblings are always associated with their beloved Grasmere, and they lived for many years in Dove Cottage, on the outskirts of the village. In 1799, William took Coleridge to see the new home he had fallen in love with and, shortly afterwards Dorothy received a letter containing the following words:

You can feel what I cannot cannot express for myself — how deeply I have been impressed by a world of scenery absolutely new to me. At Rydal and Grasmere I received I think the deepest delight ... It was to me a vision of a fair country.
Samuel Taylor Coleridge

Coniston Water and Old Man
FROM BRANTWOOD

The names of Coniston and its surrounding area hark back 1000 years, to a time of Scandinavian settlers and their Norse language. The word Coniston means town of the king and the mountain now named Old Man comes from the Norse words for pile of stones. Coniston's Old Man Mountain is the highest of all Coniston's fells and the village of Coniston lies protected beneath its shade.

Brantwood, from where this photograph was taken, is reputed to have one of the finest views in England, with roving aspects over Coniston Water and Coniston Fells. John Ruskin, who spent the happiest years of his life at Brantwood and died in the house, chose to be buried in Coniston, at St Andrew's church, in preference to London's Westminster Abbey, the accepted burial place of revered English writers. The Abbey has an area called Poets' Corner which is specially designated for these illustrious tombs. Many famous writers, including Charles Dickens, are buried there.

Ann Tyson's Cottage
HAWKSHEAD

In this small cottage, one of literature's greatest poets spent many of his most formative years: William Wordsworth lodged here with the owner, Ann Tyson, while he was a pupil at Hawkshead Grammar School (1779–1787). It is situated on a quiet, narrow lane within the old village of Hawkshead. The grammar school still stands in the centre of the village, though it is no longer used as a school. Today it is a museum, complete with the desk at which William Wordsworth sat and carved his initials.

Ann Tyson's cottage is a typical Lakeland building with a stone porch, slate roof – no doubt made with stone from one of the local quarries – and whitewashed walls. Today it still retains the alluring appeal

it had in the days of Wordsworth's happy childhood, here pictured with brilliant roses growing over the door.

Hawkshead itself is one of the Lake District's most eye-catching villages. Its cobbled squares, welcoming pubs and ancient houses help to retain an atmosphere of old world gentility with the breath of its most famous scholar still whispering on the breeze.

Azaleas in Bloom
BRANTWOOD

*The purest and most thoughtful minds are those
which love colour the most.*

John Ruskin

Brantwood was the much-loved home of the nineteenth-century aesthete, writer and art historian, John Ruskin. Ruskin was born in London in 1819, the only child of doting parents. The family travelled extensively through Europe, filling the adolescent John with a great love of Italy – Venice in particular.

Ruskin is best known for his epic work *Modern Painters*, the first volume of which was published in 1843. He also wrote the impressive tomes, *The Seven Lamps of Architecture*, *The Stones of Venice*, *Praeterita* and many lectures on art and architecture. Ruskin was a fervent moralist and religious aesthete. He believed strongly in the axiom of art and morality being firmly intertwined. He was a strong champion of the pre-Raphaelites and Turner (at the time all controversial artists) and vehemently anti-Whistler. Ruskin's favoured architectural style was Gothic.

John Ruskin died at Brantwood in 1900, just one year before England's Queen Victoria.

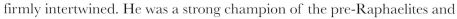

MAGNIFICENT HOMES

A long and fascinating history has provided Lakeland with a great many wonderful homes. Castles and halls in varying states of repair range from Pendragon Castle's magnificent ruins to the wonderful art gallery housed in Abbot's Hall.

Sizergh Castle
NEAR KENDAL

The stately Sizergh Castle, complete with grand park, is sited just two miles outside Kendal. It has a fourteenth-century pele (or peel) tower and additions dating from Tudor and Elizabethan times. A pele tower is a defensive structure and the one at Sizergh was built to defend the castle from Scottish attacks, a common event in the Middle Ages. The interior features several finely carved ornamentals above many of the castle's grand fireplaces – these are reputedly the best Elizabethan carvings to be found anywhere. The castle has wonderfully laid-out gardens dating back to the eighteenth century, including one of the country's largest limestone rockeries.

Sizergh Castle has been the ancestral home of the Strickland family for over 750 years and is now cared for by the National Trust. The Stricklands are devout Catholics and have always been royalists. During the Civil War they were renowned for their loyalty to the royal Stuarts and it was a Strickland warrior who carried the banner of St George at the Battle of Agincourt in 1415.

Pendragon Castle
MALLERSTANG VALLEY

The ruins of this splendid twelfth-century castle are all that remain of a once spectacular structure. According to legend, Pendragon Castle was built as a defensive pele tower by the great warrior Uther Pendragon, a man fabled throughout history to be the father of the elusive King Arthur.

In the seventeenth century, Pendragon was restored by Lady Anne Clifford. Lady Anne was a remarkable woman; at a time when property was automatically passed on through the male line, regardless of age, she fought a furious battle to inherit her father's wealth, staking her claim as his eldest child. Even more remarkable was the fact that she won. Having inherited the large estate, Lady Anne set about restoring the properties, including Pendragon and Brougham Castles. Her restorations also spread to other counties, particularly Yorkshire.

A compassionate Christian, Lady Anne also restored several churches and a hospital and paid for the building of almshouses around the Lake District. In the 1640s she built the Appleby almshouses, specifically for widows.

Lady Anne was also renowned for her gratitude for other people's kindness. Those who showed kindness towards her received an oak door lock, engraved with her initials and a key. To this day there are about eight Lady Anne door locks still intact on Lake District doors.

Rampside Hall
NEAR BARROW-IN-FURNESS

Rampside Hall, at Cumbria's southernmost tip, was built and lived in by John Knipe and his family in the seventeenth century. The Knipes were a prominent local family and fervent royalists, who fought for King Charles's Cavaliers in the Battle of Preston during the English Civil War of the 1600s.

As can be seen in this photograph, the house has many mullioned windows providing each of the hall's rooms with the maximum amount of natural light. However, until relatively recent renovations began, many of the windows were covered up and none of the locals even knew they existed. This seemingly perverse action had taken place during the period that a 'window tax' was levied. This hefty tax was payable on every window in a building, and lasted for over 150 years, from 1695 to 1851. Another startling feature of the house is its spine of 12 chimneys in the middle of the roof. These earned Rampside Hall its local nickname of 'the 12 apostles'.

In 1855 a localized earthquake destroyed one of Rampside Hall's neighbouring houses. Fortunately the hall fared rather better, suffering just a large crack along the outside wall.

Brougham Castle
NEAR PENRITH

Brougham Castle (pronounced 'Broom') is perfectly sited on the banks of the River Eamont. Built during the twelfth and thirteenth centuries, the castle is a testament to many fascinating chapters in British history including the restorations of the zealous seventeenth-century restorer, Lady Anne Clifford. The road that leads to the castle was the site of Lady Anne's final goodbye to her mother, the Countess of Cumberland, in the first part of the seventeenth century. The spot at which the two ladies bade one another farewell is marked by the Countess Pillar, a memorial placed there by the wishes of Lady Anne in 1656.

Not far from the castle is the site of an ancient Roman fort, Brocavum. The fort stands at one end of the Roman High Street, a road which runs, at great altitude, between Brocavum and the fort at Ambleside. Brougham Castle now houses some of the most important tombstones from this Roman now-ruined settlement.

Holker Hall
NEAR CARK

For almost 400 years, Holker Hall has been a family home, passed down through generations and never bought or sold. Originally owned by the Prestons, the home passed from the Prestons through intermarriage to the Lowther family and their descendants. Today the hall is owned by Lord Cavendish and his family.

Within Holker Hall are magnificent works of art, including a portrait of the English king, Charles II. There is an elegant library replete with wondrous literary tomes, an entire room filled with Wedgwood jasper ware and hence known as the Wedgwood Dressing Room, and a marvellous, twisting wooden grand staircase. There is also a bedroom in which Queen Mary slept before the Second World War.

Although its interior is striking, the most magnificent aspect of the property is its land. The formal and informal gardens encompass 25 acres. Much of the formal garden was landscaped by the renowned Inigo Jones, and a statue of him gazes out over his work. There is also a rose garden, man-made cascading waterfalls and a meadow of wild flowers – a haven for butterflies. Surrounding all this is a 125-acre deer park.

Gardens of Levens Hall
NEAR KENDAL

In response to Scottish raiders, a Pele tower was built in 1300 by the De Redmans. This was later improved and expanded to become a beautiful Elizabethan mansion with internationally famous gardens.

The first hint of what awaits are the extraordinary shapes that appear above the high garden wall alongside the road to Kendal.

On entering the garden, you are confronted by a feast of topiary. Box and yew borders, formal beds and fanciful shapes, fantastic creatures, pyramids, crowns and fowl demand your attention. Reputed to be the finest of its kind in England, it has altered little since 1690 when it was designed by Monsieur Beaumont, the French gardener of James II.

The owner of Levens Hall at that time was Colonel Grahame, a Yorkshireman who had been in the service of James II and whose favour at court declined when the king left to take up residence in France. Knowing Monsieur Beaumont's much admired garden at Hampton Court, Colonel Grahame employed Monsieur Beaumont for forty years, during which he designed the formal garden, planted a magnificent oak avenue and landscaped the parkland.

Kendal Castle
KENDAL

Not far from Kendal's town centre is Castle Hill, at the top of which can be seen the ruins of the once wealthy Kendal Castle, built in the thirteenth century. This Norman castle was the family home of the Parr family, most notably that of Sir Thomas Parr in the sixteenth century. This branch of the Parr family gained historical fame through their daughter, Catherine, who was born in 1512. On 12 July 1543, she married the English king Henry VIII.

The luckiest of his six wives, Catherine Parr was neither divorced nor beheaded. She was the last of Henry's six wives and survived him, living for a year after his death. She died in 1548, at the age of 36, having been widowed three times in her short life. The family chapel of the Parrs can be found inside Kendal Parish Church, a large, thirteenth-century church that stands in the town centre, not far from the River Kent. Visitors to the church are awestruck by the splendour of the interior, with its magnificent avenues of stone pillars and arches.

Abbot's Hall Art Gallery
KENDAL

This art gallery derives its name from its location – it stands on the site of a one-time abbot's hall. In the 1750s, the present building was begun by Colonel George Wilson, a local man who had made his money from the Kendal wool trade. Wilson and his wife lived in Abbot's Hall for just six years and since that time, the hall has never seen a continuous period of occupancy.

In 1900 the local council turned Abbot's Hall into offices. During the Second World War it was used as a home for evacuees and later became a dental practice. By 1952 it was derelict and would have fallen into ruins were it not for the Lake District Art Galleries and Museums Trust, which turned it into the wonderful gallery one can see today.

Abbot's Hall is sited on the bank of the River Kent and is overlooked by the ruins of Kendal Castle. It is one of only three independent art galleries in Britain and home to some of the eighteenth century's most inspiring works of art. Its founding principle was the belief that eighteenth-century and contemporary art are complementary and the gallery houses a spectacular collection of eighteenth-century portraiture, alongside much modern British work. It also has the largest collection of the works of George Romney anywhere in the world, including his masterpiece, 'The Gower Family'.

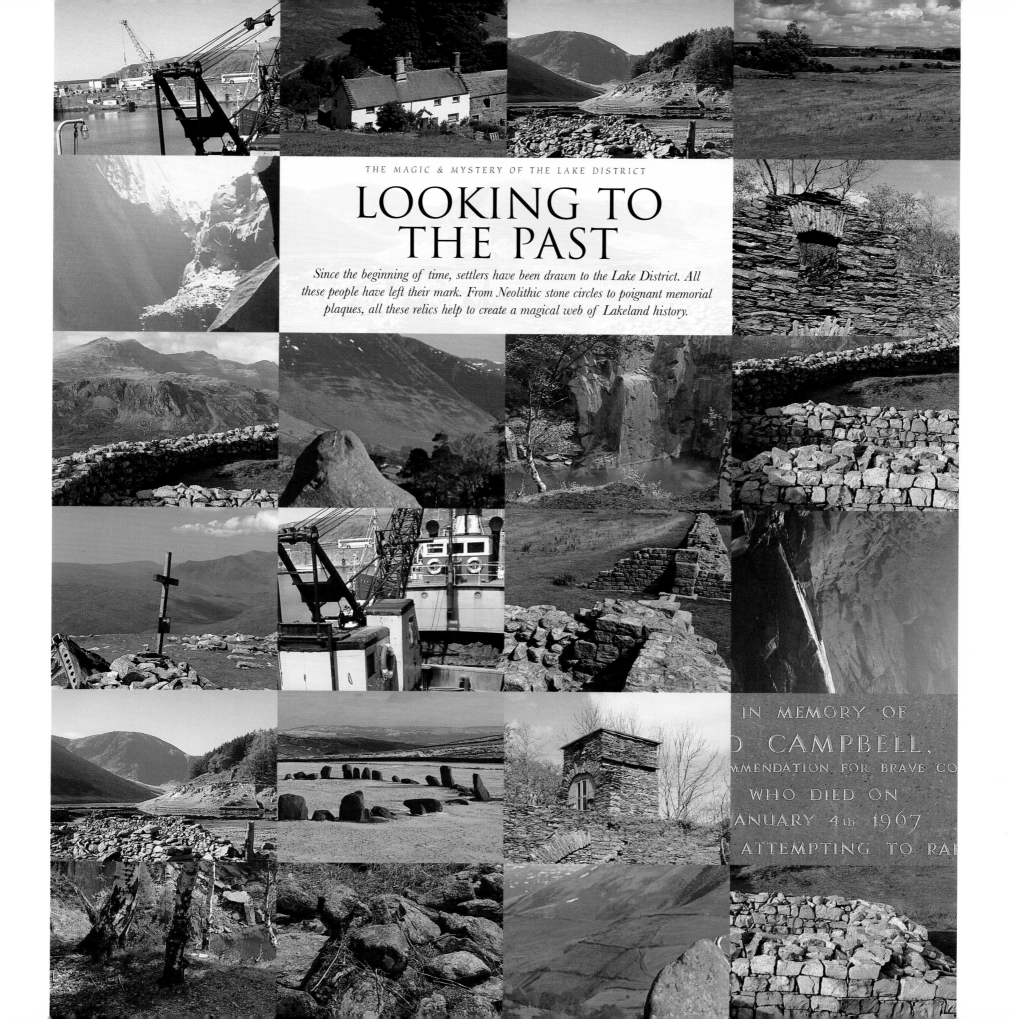

LOOKING TO THE PAST

Since the beginning of time, settlers have been drawn to the Lake District. All these people have left their mark. From Neolithic stone circles to poignant memorial plaques, all these relics help to create a magical web of Lakeland history.

IN MEMORY OF

D CAMPBELL,

MMENDATION FOR BRAVE CO

WHO DIED ON

ANUARY 4th 1967

ATTEMPTING TO RA

Castlerigg Stone Circle
NEAR KESWICK

Castlerigg's spectacular stone circle dates back to the Neolithic period. The circle is actually two circles set one within the other – the circumference of the outer circle measures over 30 metres. The reason for the circle's construction is shrouded in mystery, several theories have been put forward, but nothing definite has ever been proved. The area was almost certainly used for religious purposes but what the traditions were, or, indeed, to which religion they belonged, is uncertain.

Archaeologists are also confident that Castlerigg was used regularly as a meeting point. It appears to have been a trading place for stone axes – the Lake District was a prolific producer of axes in the Neolithic era and much local evidence of axe 'factories' has been found. The location of Castlerigg made it a strategic meeting place for the people of Lakeland and North-East England.

Rearing up from behind Castlerigg is Blencathra, the mountain whose exceptional shape has earned it the nickname of 'saddleback'. Coleridge wrote the following sonnet to one of Lakeland's most 0distinctive mountains:

On stern Blencathra's perilous height
The winds are tyrannous and strong:
And flashing forth unsteady light
From stern Blencathra's skiey height,
As loud the torrents throng!

Samuel Taylor Coleridge

Halifax Bomber Memorial
GREAT CARRS

On 22 October 1944, a Halifax bomber set off on a night-navigational exercise. It flew from RAF Topcliffe, Yorkshire, over the fells of the Lake District. Heavy cloud clothed the mountains and the bomber got lost. In an attempt to locate their position the aircraft descended, crashing into Great Carrs, a 780-metre tall mountain north of Coniston. All eight crew were killed. A simple cross and commemorative plaque marks the point of impact. The bulk of the plane dropped into Greenburn Valley.

When RAF Wyton in Cambridgeshire decided to set up a Pathfinder museum dedicated to the airmen and women of the Second World War, it seemed appropriate to include an engine and propeller boss

from the site. Of the four Merlin engines one had 'disappeared' from the fell but in 1997 a Chinook helicopter was able to lift one for RAF Wyton, and another for the Ruskin Museum at Coniston. The third remains untouched.

Those seven Canadians and their British comrade are not forgotten, for each November poppies can be found in this high place.

Glencoyne Farm
ULLSWATER

Described by Wordsworth as:

a little recess called Glencoin, where lurks a single house,
yet visible from the road – the building and objects round
them are romantic and picturesque.

William Wordsworth

A hard-working small estate is probably a more accurate description but outwardly Glencoyne does present a charming picture.

The house was built by the Howard family in the seventeenth century as a Statesman's home. The prosperity of the family is evident from the design and size of the building and the furnishings. The interior has much excellent joinery – worthy of note are two spice cupboards with carved doors, heavily burned balusters on the stairs, an enormous thick oak-planked table and a studded front door. A plaster panel in the main bedchamber bears the date 1629 and the initials of the Howards. Outside are two large cylindrical chimneys, a porch and crow-stepped gables. The latter, however, are additions from a later date.

The area around Glencoyne was a medieval deer park. Later sheep, cattle and a few pigs were kept. An average farm had 100 sheep – there were over six times as many here. Sheep are still of prime importance and the workings of the farm may be observed at various open days.

Early British Grave
NEAR DUDDON VALLEY

High on the fells, just a couple of miles from Duddon Valley, lies a grave dating from the Bronze Age. It is located on the southern slopes of Mount Caw on the ancient route which linked Duddon to Broughton-in-Furness, an impressive fell looming up to 529 metres.

During the Bronze Age most settlements were to be found at high altitude as the valleys, so lush and accommodating today, were a mass of dense, impenetrable woodland, home to packs of wolves and other dangerous beasts. It was not until the people had created tools powerful enough to deal with dense woodland that they began to venture towards lower ground.

This particular grave was robbed during the nineteenth century, but there is still plenty to satisfy the curiosity of archaeologists. They believe that the body in the grave, laid carefully in the foetal position, is possibly that of a chieftain. The evidence that suggests this is the presence of a large stone marking the grave denoting an occupant of importance.

Swinside Stone Circle
NEAR BROUGHTON-IN-FURNESS

Swinside Stone Circle is a haunting reminder of a past era. It is one of many stone circles in England, all of which taunt the twentieth-century dweller with their enigmatic history. Although many theories have been postulated as to their purpose, it is impossible to know for certain which, if any, of them are correct as no conclusive evidence has ever been uncovered. Many researchers believe that stone circles, such as this one, are the remains of a bygone astrological chart; most believe that the circles had some kind of religious significance. There is a possibility that Swinside was used for Druid rituals, as is believed of Stonehenge, in Wiltshire. Alternatively they could have been placed for use in pagan rituals, or simply to mark the site of an important event.

Broughton-in-Furness was once the home of Branwell Brontë, the artist brother of the more famous Charlotte, Emily and Anne Brontë. The Brontë family lived in Haworth, Yorkshire, an area accessible by stage coach from the Lake District.

Cathedral Cavern
LITTLE LANGDALE

Many fellsides hold secrets of the past in their huge caverns and narrow twisting tunnels that contained the green slates so sought after as building materials.

Inside the mountains, men followed the natural fissures hacking out blocks of slate with their picks. After 1760 explosives were used to extract the rock from the face, but men still had to guide the slate-bearing sledges down the fellside and trudge back up to the quarry many times a day. A covered mine such as this was riddled with access tunnels and working levels. The men worked by tallow candlelight. The installation of lighting and compressed air drills has been relatively recent.

First using pack horses and boats, then on branch lines from the new railways, the slate made its way to the industrial towns of the North and Midlands to roof the new red brick buildings of the eighteenth and nineteenth century.

Abandoned workings and their extensive spoil heaps and derelict buildings are encroached upon by trees and water which soften their outlines and mask the scale of these enormous monuments to the quarrymen.

Drowned Village
MARDALE

In times of drought the spectral remains of Mardale are revealed and explored by hordes of visitors who feel they are entering the forbidden past.

Descending the steep valley side from the road in an area known as Mardale Green, drystone walls guide them down the lane to Chapel Bridge. A little further on, the village proper was sited on the hillside, its focus – a tiny church. All that remains now are piles of stones and the sawn stumps of ancient yew trees.

Once this was an unspoilt and beautiful valley approached by a road from Brampton. The original lake covered an area only one third the size of Haweswater Reservoir, which has replaced it. Manchester Corporation gained permission to build a dam and flood the area in 1919, and the building proper began in 1934. The Dun Bull Inn was the last building in the valley and from there a walled track led walkers over the fells to Kentmere or Longsleddale. Fortunately these high areas remain untouched, but the inn was replaced by a hotel above the flood waters.

Until the eighteenth century no burials were authorized in the valley. Corpses had to be carried over the corpse road to Shap. After the last church service in 1935 the need for re-burial meant these journeys were made once more.

Farms were demolished and the tiny school building dismantled and rebuilt above the encroaching waters. People left their homes but not their memories. The village of Mardale still lives on.

Old Quarry
NEAR CONISTON

Many hundreds of millions of years ago, this area of the Lake District was filled with active volcanoes. The residue left over from volcanic activity formed the slate for which the region has now become famed and which was mined so extensively at this quarry. The volcanoes of England are now dormant and have remained so for hundreds of millennia, today they stand as mountains – enormous monuments to an almost forgotten time when the world had never known a human presence.

The area around Coniston has long been a popular place. The Romans settled here, followed a few centuries later, by the Norsemen. Today it is a much-loved tourist attraction with its many literary associations and beautiful surrounding landscape. Here a glade of exquisite trees covers the quarry and works area, enticing people to walk here. Quarries, however, are dangerous places and visitors, particularly those to whom the site is unknown, must be extremely careful when exploring the area.

Duddon Furnace
DUDDON

Duddon Furnace enjoys an idyllic woodland setting. Although a man-made structure, it has been cleverly conceived to make the most of its location. As a scheduled ancient monument, probably the most important site of charcoal iron smelting in Britain, it is worthy of admiration.

Built in 1736 the furnace was worked by six men working twelve hour shifts. Enormous barns holding stores of charcoal and iron ore are located at the highest point on the site above the furnace. It was the task of two men to ensure supplies of these materials to two others who charged the furnace from above.

The keeper of the furnace and his assistant watched the process carefully. The resulting molten metal flowed into moulds where it was marked, dated and stamped. Some iron was cast at the site, but about a quarter went to forges to be refined for local use. The furnace consumed eleven acres of woodland a week. Wood shortages caused difficulties with production. It closed in 1876, never having worked at full capacity.

Steam Dredger
WHITEHAVEN

The *Clearway* is an excellent name for a dredger. For 60 years this boat has cleared a way for vessels entering Whitehaven Harbour. Built at Aberdeen in 1927 by Hall Russell, she was fitted with a triple expansion reciprocating steam engine, with a coal boiler capable of producing 350 horsepower. After a year on the Thames she was purchased by the Whitehaven Board of Harbour Commissioners and put to use in the harbour. The task of keeping a channel open for ships carrying phosphate rock to a nearby factory kept the vessel busy until 1992.

After 1992 Morocco was able to export phosphates as phosphoric acid in tankers of 10,000 tons. These boats were too big for Whitehaven so were re-routed to nearby Workington. The remaining fishing boats do not find the harbour bar a problem. The *Clearway* has become redundant. From being the last working steam dredger she has become an object of interest to those who wish to conserve her. The spectre of the breaker's yard looms.

Tom Storey
SAWREY HAWKSHEAD

Beatrix Potter lived at Sawrey. She took a keen interest in farming, managing her own farms and being an enthusiast of Herdwick sheep. When she bought Troutbeck Park Farm in 1924 she made exhaustive enquiries to find just the right man to be her shepherd. There were 2000 acres with hundreds of sheep. So good a shepherd was Tom Storey that at the age of 30 he was in charge of the sheep on a large sheep farm in Kentmere. She offered to double Tom's wages if he would work for her.

They formed a good relationship for Tom also favoured the Herdwick breed. In 1927 Beatrix asked him to move to

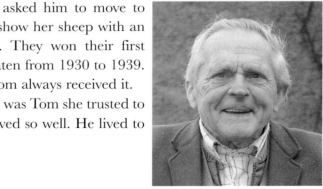

Hill Top, at Sawrey, to breed and show her sheep with an inducement of £1 on his wages. They won their first trophy a year later and were unbeaten from 1930 to 1939. If the prize was a silver tankard, Tom always received it.

When Beatrix died in 1943 it was Tom she trusted to scatter her ashes on the fells she loved so well. He lived to the age of 90 and died in 1986.

Donald Campbell's Memorial Plaque
CONISTON

Donald Campbell was a heroic figure: an inventor with an intrepid sense of adventure. His self-imposed mission was to hold the world's water speed record. Once he had attained the honour, he constantly pushed himself to new heights, breaking his own world records time and again. On 23 July 1955, at the age of 34, Campbell broke the existing water speed record in his own magnificent craft, *Bluebird*. The record-breaking event took place in the Lake District, on Ullswater, where Campbell reached an average speed of 202.32 mph. In November of the same year, he

beat his own record, also in *Bluebird*, in the US, where his average speed was 216.2 mph. In 1959 Donald travelled to Australia to try for a new world record. He succeeded, reaching an average speed of 276.33 mph.

In 1967, Donald Campbell returned to the Lake District, this time to Coniston Water. On 4 January he was killed while attempting to break his Australian record. The jet-powered *Bluebird* left the water's surface at over 270 mph and cruelly crashed back down on to the lake. This memorial plaque marks the area in which he was killed – a fond remembrance of a remarkable man.

Hardknott Roman Fort
NEAR DUDDON

Hardknott Fort, seen here with Scafell Pike in the background, is a masterpiece of Roman engineering. Known to the Romans as Mediobogdum, it was built as a strategic defence building to safeguard England's conquerors from marauding locals and attacks from nearby Scotland – the only part of the British mainland the Romans had been unable to conquer.

The fort has been dated back to some time around the first century AD and was one of a string of forts stretching from Ravenglass to Hadrian's Wall. It seems to have been abandoned by the Romans within the same century, though the reasons for this are unknown. At the time of its use, Hardknott housed 500 soldiers. Incorporated into the design were barracks, the commandant's quarters, bath houses, a granary and a parade ground.

Today visitors to Hardknott can see just the remaining stones of a once spectacular structure. Its location affords wonderful views of the Eskdale Valley and across to Scafell.

Birdoswald Roman Fort
CARLISLE

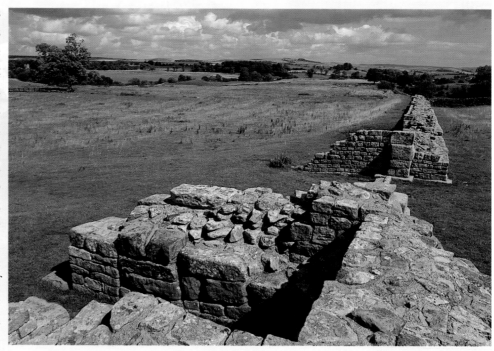

The fort at Birdoswald is one of several wall forts built by the Romans sometime around the first century AD. It is sited on the Cumbria section of Hadrian's Wall. The wall was built by the Roman Emperor Hadrian after he accepted that the Roman Empire would not be able to defeat the Scots and annex their country, an area the Romans called Caledonia. Hadrian ordered the wall to be built to show a clear line of demarcation between the Roman Empire and the land of the barbarians.

Work on the wall was begun in AD122 and completed in AD127. It stretched for 70 miles, spanning the island from the Solway Firth (not far from present-day Carlisle) and the Tyne River, the site of present-day Newcastle.

Hadrian's Wall was heavily manned by soldiers stationed at forts such as Birdoswald. A fort was placed at every mile along the way and guarded fiercely to prevent any Scottish attempt to seize control of proud Rome's new territory.

The Lake District Past and Present

This map of the area around the Lake District was drawn up by one of the foremost English cartographers of the early seventeenth century. The drawing, by map-maker John Speed, appeared in his book entitled *Theatre of the Empire of Great Britaine*, published in *c.* 1611–12. The map evokes a time when present-day Cumbria was made up of four counties: Cumberland *(Cumberlande)* and Westmorland *(Westmoreland)* with parts of Lancashire *(Lancaster)* and Yorkshire *(Yorkshire)*.

Ambleside
27, 78, 79, 115
Appleby
96, 170
Armboth
154
Askham
72
Borrowdale
20, 28, 119, 124, 134, 135
Brathay
24
Buttermere
41, 77, 116
Carlisle
195
Cartmel
64, 65, 173
Cockermouth
69, 151
Coniston
32, 35, 45, 56, 57, 90, 91, 94, 103, 144,
157, 159, 163, 165, 189, 193
Derwentwater
113, 117, 132, 133
Duddon
43, 95, 118, 130, 137, 184, 190, 194
Furness
39, 42, 46, 66, 98, 171, 185

Gosforth
63
Grange-over-Sands
14, 76, 88, 129
Grasmere
60, 89, 121, 142, 150, 162
Great Carrs
182
Grizedale
152, 153
Hawkshead
21, 53, 74, 164, 192
Kendal
34, 36, 47, 75, 93, 168, 174, 176, 177
Keswick
136, 141, 160, 180,
Kirkby Lonsdale
25, 62, 86
Langdale
18, 48, 49, 55, 126, 127, 128, 140, 156,
158, 186
Lickle Valley
37
Lowick
92, 102
Lune Valley
38
Lyndale
40, 138

Mardale
188
Patterdale
120, 122, 123
Penrith
19, 68, 99, 145, 172
Rusland Valley
50
Rydal
29, 112, 125, 148
Soulby
26
St Bees
80, 110
Troutbeck
16, 17, 106, 114, 161
Ullswater
109, 183
Ulverston
83
Wasdale Head
131, 143
Whitehaven
191
Windermere
51, 52, 81, 100, 101, 108, 111, 155,
Winster
54, 82, 139

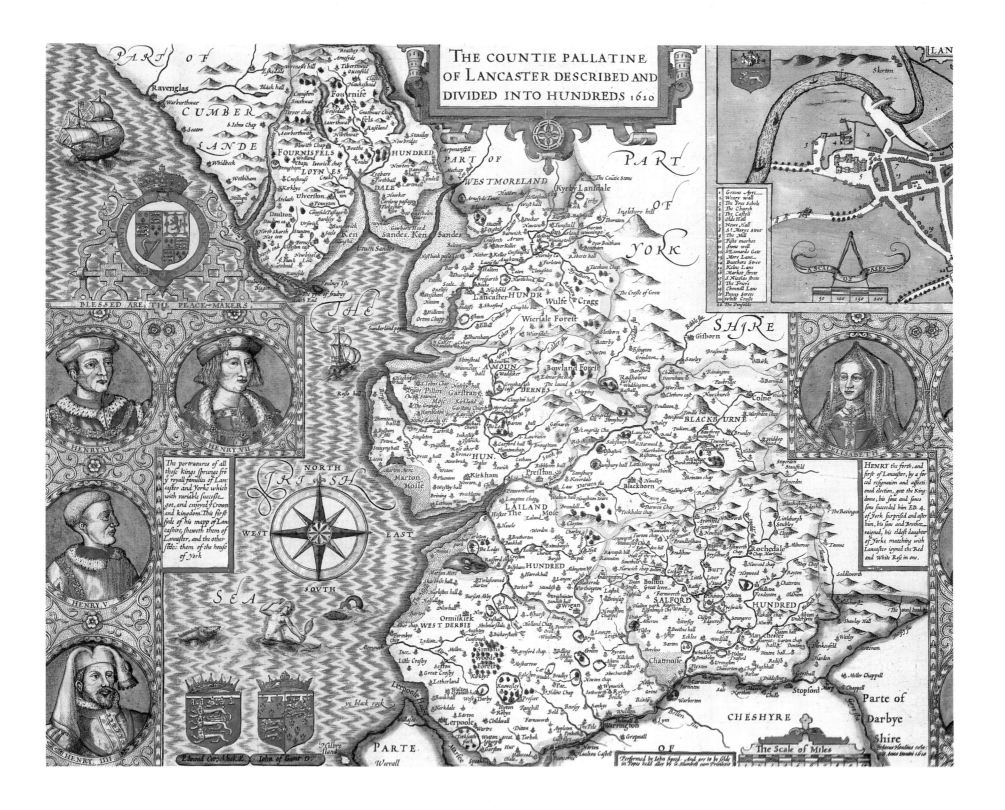

Index